SHAKESPEARE, POLITICS AND THE STATE

CONTEXT AND COMMENTARY

Series Editor: ARTHUR POLLARD

SHAKESPEARE, POLITICS AND THE STATE

Robin Headlam Wells

MACMILLAN

First published 1986

Published by
MACMILLAN EDUCATION LTD
Houndmills, Basingstoke, Hampshire RG21 2XS
and London
Companies and representatives
throughout the world

Printed in Hong Kong

British Library Cataloguing in Publication Data
Wells, Robin Headlam
    Shakespeare, politics and the State.— (Context
    and commentary)
    1. Shakespeare, William — Political and social
    views   2. Political science in literature
    I. Title   II. Series
    822.3′3   PR3017

ISBN 0–333–37590–4
ISBN 0–333–37591–2 Pbk

Contents

Acknowledgements

The author would like to thank Alison Birkinshaw who compiled the index for this book.

List of Plates

1. Encounter between European explorers and Florida Indians in 1564. Travellers' accounts of the New World stimulated debate on primitivism and the values of the civilised world.
   Photograph © Bodleian Library, Oxford.

2. Niccolo Machiavelli (1469-1527). His most famous work, *The Prince*, overturned traditional ideas about the character and virtues necessary in a good ruler.
   Photograph © Bodleian Library, Oxford.

3. Woodcut from John Foxe's *Book of Martyrs* (1554). While successive government pamphlets emphasised the terrible penalties of rebellion, radical writers continued to assert the rights of subjects to resist unjust authority.
   Photograph reproduced by kind permission of Rowlie Wymer.

4. Title page of Ralegh's providentialist *History of the World* (1614). A new generation of historians was beginning to concern itself less with the religious than with the political lessons to be learned from a study of the past.
   Photograph © The British Library.

5. The Great Chain in Being. As the traditional cosmos with its orderly system of inter-locking hierarchies began to be demolished, sceptical writers questioned the notion of a universal law of nature implanted by God in man's heart.
   Photograph © The British Library.

6. The 1985 Royal Shakespeare company production of Richard III at the Barbican with Antony Sher as the dying Richard.
   Photograph © Donald Cooper.

Note on the Texts

All passages from Shakespeare are from Peter Alexander's edition of *The Complete Works* (Collins, 1951). However, in one instance (*Richard II*, III.iii.100) I have adopted the Quarto and Folio reading 'pastors' in preference to Theobald's emendation 'pastures' which Alexander prints.

Because the Alexander text, like most modern editions of Shakespeare, is in modern spelling I have for the sake of consistency modernised the spelling and punctuation of all the documents printed with the exception of the passage from Spenser's *Faerie Queene*, which is normally printed in original spelling.

Editor's Preface

J.H. Plumb has said that 'the aim of (the historian) is to understand men both as individuals and in their social relationships in time. "Social" embraces all of man's activities – economic, religious, political, artistic, legal, military, scientific – everything, indeed, that affects the life of mankind.' Literature is itself similarly comprehensive. From Terence onwards writers have embraced his dictum that all things human are their concern.

It is the aim of this series to trace the interweavings of history and literature, to show by judicious quotation and commentary how those actually working within the various fields of human activity influenced and were influenced by those who were writing the novels, poems and plays within the several periods. An attempt has been made to show the special contribution that such writers make to the understanding of their times by virtue of their peculiar imaginative 'feel' for their subjects and the intensely personal angle from which they observe the historical phenomena that provide their inspiration and come within their creative vision. In its turn the historical evidence, besides and beyond its intrinsic importance, serves to 'place' the imaginative testimony of the writers.

The authors of the several volumes in this series have sought to intermingle history and literature in the conviction that the study of each is enhanced thereby. They have been free to adopt their own approach within the broad general pattern of the series. The topics themselves have sometimes also a particular slant and emphasis. Commentary, for instance, has had to be more detailed in some cases than in others. All the contributors to the series are at one, however, in the belief (at a time when some critics would not only divorce texts from their periods but even from their authors) that literature is the creation of actual men and women, actually living in an identifiable set of historical circumstances, themselves both the creatures and the creators of their times.

ARTHUR POLLARD

To Anne Wrightson in gratitude

Introduction

'He was not of an age, but for all time.' These famous words have been echoed by countless Shakespearean critics in a sense in which their author, Ben Jonson, probably did not intend them to be understood. It is true that, in praising Shakespeare's plays for their timeless quality, Jonson is expressing the neoclassical belief, summed up by his 18th-century namesake, that 'Nothing can please many, and please long, but just representations of general nature' (Samuel Johnson, *Preface to Shakespeare*, p.61). But it is unlikely that a satirist as topical as Ben Jonson would have shared the view – still widely held – that Shakespeare was 'interested in politics only insofar as they afforded him an opportunity of identifying himself with human characters undergoing the tugs and stresses of public life' (Palmer, *Political Characters of Shakespeare*, p.313). Shakespeare's knowledge of human nature and his skill in portraying the mechanisms of self-deception are not in dispute. But to argue that he shows an indifference to political questions in the histories and tragedies is to ignore the topicality of these plays. They are topical not in the sense of alluding to contemporary events but in the sense that they reflect and embody subjects of current debate. These plays are essentially political. They are, as Jan Kott says, about 'people involved in history' (*Shakespeare Our Contemporary*, p.16).

Contrary to the impression which E.M.W. Tillyard gave in his influential *Shakespeare's History Plays* (1944), the twenty-year period when Shakespeare wrote most of his plays was not one of intellectual uniformity, but a time of social unrest and energetic political controversy. It was ironically in the years following England's triumphant success in her first great naval battle that the country suffered the worst economic depression it had known since the Tudors came to power. The national euphoria generated by the defeat of the Spanish Armada in 1588 was short-lived. The combined effects of inflation, of crippling taxes made necessary by the continuing war with Spain, of a series of appallingly bad harvests and of new outbreaks of plague had a devastating effect on national morale. In 1596 starving workers rioted in Oxfordshire. In the following year a Norfolk grain barge was seized by the populace. In Canterbury in the same year carts loaded with grain for export were hijacked.

The boundaries with which historians demarcate their particular periods of specialisation are always to some extent arbitrary. Yet Elizabethans themselves clearly sensed that an age was coming to an end. 'All our beauty, and our trim, decays,' wrote John Donne in 1597, 'Like courts removing, or like ended plays.' The sense of national insecurity which is such a characteristic feature of the time is reflected in the emergency legislation of the 1597-8 parliaments. What is significant in this legislation is not so much the measures which were passed – they were largely designed to ameliorate the lot of the urban poor – as the role taken by the House of Commons in formulating them.

In the long-standing struggle between Elizabeth and her parliaments over the question of royal prerogative the queen had been under constant pressure from the Commons to acknowledge their right to initiate legislation. For Elizabeth it was a losing battle. But although she was increasingly unsuccessful in her attempt to exclude the Commons from what she regarded as 'matters of state' (that is, religion, foreign policy, monopolies and the problem of the succession), the House was careful not to upset a balance of power which was vital to national security. For example, when Peter Wentworth, a leading figure in the Puritan campaign for parliamentary reform, launched a particularly virulent attack on the royal prerogative in 1576 it was not the Privy Council but an embarrassed House of Commons which decided to remove him from the chamber and let him cool off in the Tower.

Like Catholic plots, the more extreme forms of Puritan agitation had the effect not of undermining but of consolidating parliamentary support for the crown. By the

1590s, however, both of these threats had lost much of their force and as the need to close ranks on religious and foreign policy became less urgent, so demand grew in the Commons for the right to initiate legislation. It is significant that when it became clear in 1597 that drastic measures were needed to remedy the country's social and economic problems, it was the House of Commons and not the government which framed the new bills. This legislation marks, in J.E. Neale's words, 'a significant advance in the "winning of initiative" by the House of Commons, which was to be the outstanding theme of the Jacobean Parliaments, and in course of time was to effect a constitutional revolution' (*Elizabeth I and her Parliaments*, Vol. II, p.337).

However, although the Commons was undoubtedly beginning to replace the Privy Council as the centre of power in Elizabethan England, there is no real analogy between the disputes of the 1590s and 1600s between crown and parliament and the conflicts of the 1630s when, for the first time, there began to emerge a truly radical Puritan opposition. Friction between Elizabeth and James and their parliaments took place within the context of a conservative desire on both sides to preserve the existing order. One of the issues which had caused the Elizabethan Commons most frustration was monopolies, a question on which Elizabeth stubbornly refused to yield her prerogative. Originally designed as a form of protective patent, monopolies had by the end of the century become in effect a system of perquisites handed out to officials and courtiers whom the queen wanted to reward. The issue came to a head in 1601 when the Commons angrily demanded a wholesale reform of the monopolies system. Yet when Elizabeth capitulated, the Commons made no attempt to capitalise on its victory. Instead of using its advantage to press for further constitutional reform, it offered the queen a deputation of thanks.

With Elizabeth's death the uneasy relations between crown and parliament became even more strained as James declared his belief in the divine authority of kings and the Commons reasserted its right to formulate policy. Matters came to a head once more in 1604-5 when debate on the question of purveyance (the requisitioning of provisions for the royal household) became so heated that for a time all London waited eagerly for news of the day's parliamentary exchanges. When a bill for the restraint of purveyance was drawn up by parliamentary committee James declared that this was an intolerable invasion of his prerogative. The authors of the bill, John Hare and Lawrence Hyde, replied in equally uncompromising terms. So inflammatory were their attacks on the king that Hare and Hyde were compared with the tribunes of republican Rome (Zeeveld, 'Coriolanus and Jacobean Politics', pp.327-8). As one contemporary observer wrote, 'Hyde yielded many reasons why we should not yield more unto the King than we did; with many invectives, and so far put the house in distaste, as that expectation grew of the sequel. And if your lordship had heard them, you would have said that Hare and Hyde had represented the tribunes of the people' (Birch, *The Court and Times of James the First*, Vol. I, p.60).

But once again a potentially explosive situation was defused. James, recognising the need for conciliation, remained calm in the face of these attacks and eventually Hyde was persuaded to moderate his language in what amounted to an apology to the Lords.

In James' first parliament power was undoubtedly shifting towards the Commons but mounting pressure for constitutional reform should not be interpreted as a demand for the kind of republican constitution which Shakespeare portrays in *Coriolanus*. Hare and Hyde may have been popularly compared with the tribunes of republican Rome but, unlike Sicinius and Brutus in Shakespeare's play, their constituency was not the populace as a whole but the House of Commons. What Hare and Hyde were demanding was not sovereignty of the people but increased legislative rights for the House of Commons. Only with the pamphlet debates of the middle years of the 17th century does popular demand for individual rights and liberties begin to be articulated. Although Shakespeare writes about societies in crisis it would be wrong to see the assassinations, the coups and the revolutions he portrays as reflections of a contemporary democratic radicalism. In Shakespeare's lifetime not even the most vociferous critics of the monarchy advocated universal suffrage. To have done so would have been illogical. In the

1590s and 1600s conservatives and radicals almost without exception appealed in their writings to a view of the universe and of human nature which would have made the kind of revolutionary egalitarianism that appeared in the 1640s and '50s unthinkable. The fact that Elizabethan writers do not share our axiomatic belief in democracy does not of course mean that they accepted without question establishment doctrines of authority. To avoid anachronistic readings of Shakespeare the modern student must begin, as Elizabethans themselves did, with the debate on human nature (Chapter 1).

The Renaissance inherited from the Middle Ages a theory of cosmos which had its origins in ancient Greek philosophy. Of the various metaphors commonly used to express the order and rationality of the universe, the most familiar is the Chain of Being. This prototypal image of multiformity reduced to unity is rarely absent from medieval and Renaissance discussions of world order and was not finally abandoned as a model for social and personal harmony until the middle of the 18th century. But the Chain of Being was not simply a static symbol of world order; for Renaissance humanists it was a dynamic image expressive of the individual's potential for either amelioration or degeneration. Classical and Christian writers both describe the prelapsarian world as a time when human passions were naturally held in check by reason. However, at the Fall humanity lost its natural temper with the consequence that it now occupied a unique position in the universal scheme of things, still retaining elements of a former god-like reason yet sharing with the beasts a propensity to obey natural impulses. But if human nature was susceptible of improvement, it was only through the discipline of civilised life that the effects of the Fall could be repaired.

Although, as the documents extracted in Chapter 1 show, this traditional view of human nature was subject to radical criticism from both religious and secular thinkers in the 16th century, political pamphleteers continued on the whole to base their arguments on familiar premises (Chapter 2). In debating the relative merits of monarchies, aristocracies and democracies Elizabethan writers appealed to the principle of analogy. The essential unity of the universe was apparent from the fact that the same principles of order operated on every plane of existence. Just as one god ruled the universe, so it followed by analogy that one man must rule the state; or to turn the analogy round, as reason should control man's lower faculties, so the inferior members of society should be governed by a single figure of authority. But while conservatives claimed that absolute monarchy was the only natural form of government, writers anxious to limit the powers of the crown argued in support of a mixed constitution which embodied all three types of government, though even the latter argument claimed to be based on the laws of nature. One point on which both critics and apologists of the Tudor monarchy were agreed, however, was the uncertainties and dangers of democracy. Critical as Shakespeare is of rulers who abuse the trust placed in them as guardians of social order, he makes it clear that democracy is no answer to the problems of a society divided against itself. Exploited the plebeians undoubtedly are in a play like *Coriolanus* but, as Elizabethan writers never tire of reminding us, an innately feckless and indecisive populace is not to be trusted with political power.

Irrespective of whether or not it was accepted that the principle of monarchy was sanctioned by an indubitable law of nature, in practice national welfare in Reformation England was closely dependent on the wisdom and astuteness of the king or queen. It is not surprising, therefore, that much political discussion in the 16th century was concerned with the character of the ideal ruler (Chapter 3). To the medieval mind a king was to be seen as God's deputy on earth, ruling with the same loving care that a father showed for his family and expecting in return the obedience and respect of his subjects. Such a view of kingship was highly convenient to the Tudors, faced as they were with the problems of a disputed right to the throne and, after 1534, of establishing a semblance of national unity on the emotive question of religion. But while pro-establishment writers continued to appeal to the medieval conception of kingship, it was clear that qualities other than benevolence and integrity were necessary for survival in the dangerous world of Reformation politics. In Shakespeare's most successful ruler, Henry V, can be seen a new and at times ruthless political realism which owes much to the writings of Machiavelli.

Elizabethan political thought represents an amalgam of medieval theories of society modified by the particular problems of a Reformation state. The simile so widely employed by 16th-century writers in which the state is compared to a living organism, all of whose parts contribute to the welfare of the whole body, was traditional. However, the doctrine of absolute obedience to the crown which is such a distinctive feature of Tudor political theory was something new (Chapter 4). After the chaos of the Wars of the Roses a return to powerful monarchy was welcomed by a rising trading class, for whom social stability was a paramount concern. With the break from Rome in 1534 the need for strong central government became even more imperative. Having rebelled against established authority itself, the Henrician regime had to guard against counter-reform by measures designed to minimise the threat of rebellion. In an age when religion aroused stronger feelings than any other public issue, the most effective way to do this was to emphasise the sin of disobedience. That the state's publicly proclaimed doctrine of non-resistance received such widespread acceptance is a measure of the success of the new monarchy. However, that is not to say that its official propaganda went unchallenged. From the 1530s onwards a small but steady stream of dissident writers had reasserted the medieval belief in the rights of subjects to rebel against unjust authority. By the 1590s, when the threat of invasion from Catholic Europe had largely been averted, moderate opinion became increasingly sceptical of the idea, so forcibly expressed by Shakespeare's Richard II, that kings are sacrosanct. As van Baumer writes, 'Before 1588 the cult of authority was fashionable in England. After that date it became to a certain extent an object of ridicule, and was cultivated by only a minority' (*The Early Tudor Theory of Kingship*, p.90).

Assertions by some of Shakespeare's characters of the inviolability of kings must, of course, be seen in their dramatic context. In a similar way we cannot assume, when the same characters declare their belief in an avenging deity who punishes usurpers for the sin of disobedience, that these views are necessarily Shakespeare's own. Theories of history were undergoing radical change in the 16th century

(Chapter 5.) While the English chronicle sources on which Shakespeare relied for much of his historical material showed only a limited interest in political questions, the so-called 'new' historians were concerned less with the workings of providence than with the practical lessons to be learned from a study of the past. That providence performs an active role in human affairs is something which is taken for granted by many of Shakespeare's characters. But in claiming, as some critics have done, that Shakespeare endorses their belief in an avenging deity who with relentless logic punishes the wicked and rewards the virtuous, there is a danger of reducing the plays to doctrinaire theological tracts. If there is one thing which clearly emerges from Shakespeare's dramatisation of history, it is the complexities of political life and the intractability of its problems.

New interest in the human factors involved in history may be seen as one aspect of a larger tendency in the 16th century to challenge traditional theological assumptions about the basis of human societies. This involved a re-evaluation of the meaning of natural law (Chapter 6). For the conservative Elizabethan the foundations of social justice lay in hierarchical order. The fact that this principle was so widely accepted does not mean that Elizabethans were incapable of serious speculative thought. Hierarchy was a principle inscribed in the very structure of the universe; it was an axiomatic law of nature no more open to question than the circular revolutions of the planets. Yet it was precisely these things which were being questioned in the later 16th century. As the astronomers Brahe and Kepler were redrawing the map of the heavens, thinkers like Montaigne began the work of demolition which was ultimately to leave the beautiful, orderly, rational structure of the medieval cosmos in ruins. With the collapse of the old world-view, theories of natural law underwent a radical transformation. Originally signifying that system of duties and mutual obligations which defined man's place in the divinely instituted order of the universe, natural law was beginning by the 1650s to be taken to mean the inalienable rights of free and equal individuals.

However, traditional patterns of thought die hard. If Elizabethan writers were clearly conscious of the fact that they were living at a time of intellectual transition, we should be wary of attributing to them exactly those ideas which they found most threatening. Two hundred years after Shakespeare's death poets like Pope and Thomson could still appeal to the universal Chain of Being as a model for social order and expect to be understood by their readers.

Shakespeare's own position in the debate on the meaning of natural law is notoriously difficult to determine. So finely balanced are the rival points of view which form the dialectic of his plays that it is often assumed that, being primarily concerned with human character, he was indifferent to political and philosophical questions. But the balancing of one point of view or set of interests against another should not necessarily be interpreted simply as a desire for impartiality. One of Shakespeare's most characteristic techniques is to present us with evidence whose apparently self-contradictory nature makes it seem impossible for us to make a rational judgement on the character or problem concerned. An obvious example of this technique is the portrayal of characters like Antonio and Jessica in *The Merchant of Venice*. Antonio and Jessica stubbornly resist our natural wish to slot them into neat categories of good and evil, not just because we possess insufficient information about them but because the facts we are given cancel each other out. The same principle is true of more abstract problems, such as the question of natural justice in *King Lear*. In this play the characters themselves are for the most part unambiguously good or evil. What makes it so difficult to adjudicate between their mutually contradictory views of nature and the gods is that the evidence on either side seems to be so finely balanced. On one level these techniques have the effect of reproducing in the audience the dilemmas experienced by the characters on stage as they attempt to make sense of their world; on a broader level they reflect with unique fidelity 'the very age and body of the time, his form and pressure'. Shakespeare's final word on the question of human nature and the ideal society may perhaps be deduced from a comparison of the first and last extracts printed in this book. Both are from *The Tempest*, Shakespeare's last play, and both contain versions of the Golden-Age myth. What differentiates them is their status in the characters' minds. One is a daydream; the other is a vision.

1 Civilisation and the Debate on Human Nature

In *The Tempest* a royal wedding party returning to Italy from Tunis is shipwrecked on a fertile Mediterranean island. The natural beauty of their refuge inspires in one of the king's courtiers thoughts of establishing a utopian society where men and women could live virtuously in harmony with nature. But Gonzalo's primitivist view of humanity does not go unchallenged: his companions are clearly not impressed with this dream of a society where not only social inequality but even crime has been abolished.

> *Gon.* Had I plantation of this isle, my lord–
> *Ant.* He'd sow 't with nettle-seed.
> *Seb.*   Or docks, or mallows.
> *Gon.* And were the king on't, what would I do?
> *Seb.* Scape being drunk for want of wine.
> *Gon.* I' th' commonwealth I would by contraries
> Execute all things; for no kind of traffic
> Would I admit; no name of magistrate;
> Letters should not be known; riches, poverty,
> And use of service, none; contract, succession,
> Bourn, bound of land, tilth, vineyard, none;
> No use of metal, corn, or wine, or oil;
> No occupation; all men idle, all;
> And women too, but innocent and pure;
> No sovereignty–
> *Seb.*   Yet he would be king on't.
> *Ant.* The latter end of his commonwealth forgets the beginning.
> *Gon.* All things in common nature should produce
> Without sweat or endeavour. Treason, felony,
> Sword, pike, knife, gun, or need of any engine,
> Would I not have; but nature should bring forth,

Of its own kind, all foison, all abundance,
To feed my innocent people.
Seb. No marrying 'mong his subjects?
Ant. None, man; all idle; whores and knaves.
Gon. I would with such perfection govern, sir,
T' excel the golden age.
Seb.   Save his Majesty!
Ant. Long live Gonzalo!
Gon.   And – do you mark me, sir?
Alon. Prithee, no more; thou dost talk nothing to me.

The Tempest, II.i.137-164.

For once Dr Johnson was wrong when he wrote in his
Preface to Shakespeare 'the contest about the original
benevolence or malignity of man had not yet commenced'
(p.88). The Renaissance debate on human nature, to which
Gonzalo's utopian dream forms an important contribution, is
an essential element in Shakespeare's plays: indeed it would
be no exaggeration to say that it informs most 16th-century
social and political thought. The terms of the debate are set
out as clearly as anywhere in a little-known political treatise
written in the 1530s by a scholar at Henry VIII's court.
    Thomas Starkey's *Dialogue Between Pole and Lupset* is one
of the most important documents of English Renaissance
thought. At a time when social criticism was a hazardous
enterprise Starkey's book was exceptional both for its
exposure of the 'general faults and misorders and universal
decays of the commonwealth' and also for the radical nature
of the remedies it proposed. Before Starkey embarks on his
diagnosis of the ills of his society he first establishes certain
fundamental truths about human nature. His discussion takes
the form of an imaginary dialogue between two of his friends,
Reginald Pole, a diplomat at court before his conscience
drove him into exile, and a cleric named Thomas Lupset.
What divides the two is their interpretation of the social evils
they both agree in deploring. For Pole, represented by
Starkey here as a primitivist, the cause lies in the very nature
of social institutions. In particular it is city life which has
contaminated our natural virtue. But Lupset argues that, on

the contrary, it is not civilisation which has corrupted people but a flaw in human nature itself.

> *Pole.* You said last of all that man is born, and of nature brought forth, to a civility, and to live in politic order – the which thing to me seemeth clean contrary. For if you call this civility and living in politic order, a commonalty to live either under a prince or a common council in cities and towns, meseemeth man should not be born thereto, forasmuch as man at the beginning lived many years without any such policy; at the which time he lived more virtuously and more according to the dignity of his nature than he doth now in this which you call politic order and civility. We see also now in our days, those men which live out of cities and towns, and have fewest laws to be governed by, live better than others do in their goodly cities never so well built and inhabited, governed with so many laws for common. You see by experience in great cities most vice, most subtlety and craft; and, contrary, ever in the rude country most study of virtue, and very true simplicity. You see what adultery, murder and vice, what usury, craft and deceit, what gluttony and all pleasure of body is had in cities and towns, by the reason of this society and company of men together, which all in the country and rude life of them is avoided, by the reason that they live not together after your civility. Therefore if this be civil life and order – to live in cities and towns with so much vice and misorder – meseem man should not be born thereto, but rather to life in the wild forest, there more following the study of virtue, as it is said men did in the golden age wherein man lived according to his natural dignity.
>
> *Lupset.* Nay, Master Pole, you take the matter amiss. This is not the civil life that I mean – to live together in cities and towns so far out of order as it were a multitude conspiring together in vice, one taking pleasure of another without regard of honesty. But this I call the civil life, contrary: living together in good and politic order one ever ready to do good to another, and as it were conspiring together in all

virtue and honesty. This is the very true and civil life; and though it be so that man abuseth the society and company of man in cities and towns, giving himself to all vice, yet we may not therefore cast down cities and towns and drive man to the woods again and wild forests wherein he lived at the first beginning, rudely. The fault whereof is in neither the cities nor towns, nor in the laws ordained thereto, but it is in the malice of man, which abuseth and turneth that thing which might be to his wealth and felicity to his own destruction and misery – as he doth almost all thing that God and nature hath provided to him for the maintenance of his life. For how abuseth he his health, strength and beauty, his wit, learning and policy, how all manner of meats and drinks to the vain pleasure of the body; yea, and shortly to say, everything almost he abuseth. And yet things are not therefore utterly these to be cast away nor to be taken from the use of man.

And so the society and company of man is not to be accused as the cause of this misorder, but rather such as be great, wise and politic men, which fly from office and authority; by whose wisdom the multitude might be contained and kept in good order and civility – such, I say, are rather to be blamed. For like as by the persuasion of wise men in the beginning men were brought from their rudeness and bestial life to this civility so natural to man, so by like wisdom they must be contained and kept therein. Therefore, Master Pole, without any more cavillations, meseemeth it should be best for you to apply your mind to be of the number of them which study to restore this civil order and maintain this virtuous life in cities and towns, to the common utility.

Thomas Starkey, *Dialogue Between Reginald Pole and Thomas Lupset* (c.1534), pp.27-8.

Both Shakespeare's Gonzalo and Starkey's Reginald Pole appeal in support of their primitivist view of human nature to the myth of the Golden Age: in fact Gonzalo's speech owes much indirectly to Ovid's account of the four ages of the world in the first book of the *Metamorphoses*. So powerful an influence did this classic version of the Golden-Age myth have on the European imagination that its phrases continued to be echoed in poetry until at least the middle of the 18th century. The following extract is from the great Elizabethan translation of the *Metamorphoses* by Arthur Golding.

> Then sprang up first the golden age, which of it self maintained,
> The truth and right of every thing unforced and unconstrained.
> There was no fear of punishment, there was no threatening law
> In brazen tables nailed up, to keep the folk in awe.
> There was no man would crouch or creep to judge with cap in hand,
> They lived safe without a judge in every realm and land.
> The lofty pinetree was not hewn from mountains where it stood,
> In seeking strange and foreign lands to rove upon the flood.
> Men knew none other countries yet, than where themselves did keep:
> There was no town enclosed yet, with walls and ditches deep.
> No horn nor trumpet was in use, no sword nor helmet worn.
> The world was such, that soldiers help might easily be forborn.
> The fertile earth as yet was free, untouched of spade or plough,
> And yet it yielded of itself of every things enough.
> And men themselves contented well with plain and simple food,
> That on the earth by nature's gift without their travail stood,
> Did live by rasps, hips and haws, by cornels, plums and cherries,
> By sloes and apples, nuts and pears, and loathsome bramble berries,

And by the acorns dropped on ground from Jove's
    broad tree in field.
The springtime lasted all the year, and Zephyr with
    his mild
And gentle blast did cherish things that grew of own
    accord.
The ground untilled, all kind of fruits did plenteously
    afford.
No muck nor tillage was bestowed on lean and barren
    land,
To make the corn of better head and ranker for to
    stand.
Then streams ran milk, then streams ran wine, and
    yellow honey flowed
From each green tree whereon the rays of fiery
    Phoebus glowed.

> Ovid, *Metamorphoses* (c.AD 8, trans. 1565-7),
> Book I, ll.103-128.

What both Pole and Gonzalo omit from their account of
human nature is the fact that, with the passing of the
legendary Golden Age, humanity lost its natural virtue. In the
second book of *The Faerie Queene* (1590) Edmund Spenser
retells the story (based again on Ovid) of man's fall from his
primal state of innocence.

The antique world, in his first flowring youth,
    Found no defect in his Creatours grace,
    But with glad thankes, and unreproved truth,
    The gifts of soveraigne bountie did embrace:
    Like Angels life was then mens happy cace;
    But later ages pride, like corn-fed steed,
    Abusd her plenty, and fat swolne encreace
    To all licentious lust, and gan exceed
The measure of her meane, and naturall first need.

Then gan a cursed hand the quiet wombe
    Of his great Grandmother with steele to wound,
    And the hid treasures in her sacred tombe,
    With Sacriledge to dig. Therein he found

> Fountaines of gold and silver to abound,
> Of which the matter of his huge desire
> And pompous pride eftsoones he did compound;
> Then avarice gan through his veines inspire
> His greedy flames, and kindled life-devouring fire.
>
> Edmund Spenser, *The Faerie Queene* (1590-96),
> II.vii.16-17.

The pagan Golden-Age myth closely parallels the Christian myth of Eden and the Fall. It is because they believe that our post-lapsarian nature is flawed that humanists and Christians alike argue that we need the disciplining influence of civilisation to restrain and curb our fallen passions. This traditional belief in the need for the rule of civilisation is summed up by Bishop Ponet in a pamphlet entitled *A Short Treatise of Politic Power* (1556): 'As oxen, sheep, goats and other unreasonable creatures cannot for lack of reason rule themselves, but must be ruled by a more excellent creature, that is man, so man . . . because through the fall of the first man, his reason is corrupt, and sensuality hath gotten the over hand, is not able by himself to rule himself, but must needs have a more excellent governor' (Sig. Aii).

Every age evolves a characteristic terminology for articulating its fundamental intellectual preoccupations. In the 16th century the terms most widely used to debate the question of 'the original benevolence or malignity of man' were 'art' and 'nature'. If human nature is flawed by the Fall, then the arts of civilisation must be employed to remedy its imperfections. As John Dennis remarked in the 18th century, 'The great design of arts is to restore the decays that happened to human nature by the Fall, by restoring order'. In *The Arte of English Poesie* George Puttenham uses the simile of a gardener improving his stock to illustrate the principle of the transforming power of art.

> In some cases we say art is an aid and coadjutor to nature, and a furtherer of her actions to good effect, or peradventure a mean to supply her wants, by reinforcing the causes wherein she is impotent and defective, as doth the art of physic, by helping the natural concoction, retention, distribution, expulsion,

and other virtues, in a weak and unhealthy body. Or as the good gardener seasons his soil by sundry sorts of compost: as muck or marl, clay or sand, and many times by blood, or lees of oil or wine, or stale, or perchance with more costly drugs; and waters his plants, and weeds his herbs and flowers, and prunes his branches, and unleaves his boughs to let in the sun; and twenty other ways cherisheth them, and cureth their infirmities, and so makes that never, or very seldom any of them miscarry, but bring forth their flowers and fruits in season. And in both these cases it is no signal praise for the physician and gardener to be called good and cunning artificers.

In another respect art is not only an aid and coadjutor to nature in all her actions, but an alterer of them, and in some sort a surmounter of her skill, so as by means of it her own effects shall appear more beautiful or strange and miraculous, as in both cases before remembered. The physician by the cordials he will give his patient, shall be able not only to restore the decayed spirits of man, and render him health, but also to prolong the term of his life many years over and above the stint of his first and natural constitution. And the gardener by his art will not only make an herb, or flower, or fruit, come forth in his season without impediment, but also will embellish the same in virtue, shape, odour and taste, that nature of her self would never have done: as to make the single gillyflower, or marigold, or daisy, double; and the white rose, red, yellow, or carnation, a bitter melon sweet; a sweet apple, sour; a plum or cherry without a stone; a pear with core or kernel, a gourd or cucumber like to a horn, or any other figure he will, any of which things nature could not do without man's help and art. These actions also are most singular, when they be most artificial.

George Puttenham, *The Arte of English Poesie* (1589),
pp.253-4.

It is the same horticultural imagery which Shakespeare puts into the mouth of Polixenes in the fourth act of *The Winter's*

Tale. The scene is rich in dramatic irony. While Polixenes is testing Perdita's honesty he is no more aware than she is that the shepherdess who so charmingly plays the part of May Queen is in reality a foundling princess.

> *Per.* [*To Polixenes*] Sir, welcome.
> It is my father's will I should take on me
> The hostess-ship o' th' day. [*To Camillo*] You're
>   welcome, sir.
> Give me those flow'rs there, Dorcas. Reverend sirs,
> For you there's rosemary and rue; these keep
> Seeming and savour all the winter long.
> Grace and remembrance be to you both!
> And welcome to our shearing.
> *Pol.*   Shepherdess–
>   A fair one are you–well you fit our ages
> With flow'rs of winter.
> *Per.*   Sir, the year growing ancient,
> Not yet on summer's death nor on the birth
> Of trembling winter, the fairest flow'rs o' th' season
> Are our carnations and streak'd gillyvors,
> Which some call nature's bastards. Of that kind
> Our rustic garden's barren; and I care not
> To get slips of them.
> *Pol.*   Wherefore, gentle maiden,
>   Do you neglect them?
> *Per.*   For I have heard it said
> There is an art which in their piedness shares
> With great creating nature.
> *Pol.*   Say there be;
> Yet nature is made better by no mean
> But nature makes that mean; so over that art,
> Which you say adds to nature, is an art
> That nature makes. You see, sweet maid, we marry
> A gentler scion to the wildest stock,
> And make conceive a bark of baser kind
> By bud of nobler race. This is an art
> Which does mend nature–change it rather; but
> The art itself is nature.
> *Per.*   So it is.
> *Pol.* Then make your garden rich in gillyvors,

And do not call them bastards.
Per.   I'll not put
The dibble in earth to set one slip of them;
No more than were I painted I would wish
This youth should say 'twere well, and only therefore
Desire to breed by me. Here's flow'rs for you:
Hot lavender, mints, savory, marjoram;
The marigold, that goes to bed wi' th' sun,
And with him rises weeping; these are flow'rs
Of middle summer, and I think they are given
To men of middle age. Y'are very welcome.

The Winter's Tale, IV.iv.70-108.

In *The Winter's Tale* Shakespeare is concerned not so much with the relative merits of court and country values as with the question of civilised and uncivilised conduct. Paradoxically, while it is Perdita who wins our emotional sympathy in this scene with her beautiful and ingenuous deprecation of all that is unnatural, the play itself repeatedly draws attention to its own artificiality.

If human nature is susceptible of improvement through the arts of civilisation, it is also capable, as we see only too vividly in Leontes' passionate and destructive jealousy, of degenerating into barbarity. As Pico della Mirandola explains in a celebrated passage from his 'Oration on the Dignity of Man', it is man's unique position in the universal scheme of things which gives him the power either to ameliorate his fallen nature or to sink to the level of the beasts.

> At last the best of artisans ordained that the creature to whom He had been able to give nothing proper to himself should have joint possession of whatever had been peculiar to each of the different kinds of being. He therefore took man as a creature of indeterminate nature and, assigning him a place in the middle of the world, addressed him thus: 'Neither a fixed abode nor a form that is thine alone nor any function peculiar to thyself have we given thee, Adam, to the end that according to thy longing and according to thy judgement thou mayest have and possess what abode,

what form, and what functions thou thyself shalt desire. The nature of all other beings is limited and constrained within the bounds of laws prescribed by Us. Thou, constrained by no limits, in accordance with thine own free will, in whose hand We have placed thee, shalt ordain for thyself the limits of thy nature. We have set thee at the world's center that thou mayest from thence more easily observe whatever is in the world. We have made thee neither of heaven nor of earth, neither mortal nor immortal, so that with freedom of choice and with honor, as though the maker and molder of thyself, thou mayest fashion thyself in whatever shape thou shalt prefer. Thou shalt have the power to degenerate into the lower forms of life, which are brutish. Thou shalt have the power, out of thy soul's judgement, to be reborn into the higher forms, which are divine.'

> Giovanni Pico della Mirandola, 'Oration on the
> Dignity of Man'
> (1486), pp.224-5.

Like Pico, Thomas Starkey asserts the dignity of man. But while he insists that fallen humanity still possesses the faculty of right reason, he admits that with this reason 'are joined by nature so many affects [passions] and vicious desires . . . that except man with cure, diligence and labour resist to the same, they overrun reason . . . and so bring man . . . from that life which is convenient to his nature and dignity, insomuch that he is then as a brute beast' (p.152). The fatal ease with which man is capable of transforming himself into a 'brute beast' is an explicitly stated theme in *Othello*. In a scene which adumbrates the conclusion of the play's main plot Othello's Lieutenant Michael Cassio regrets his own failure to control his emotions in the drunken brawl with Roderigo.

Cas. Reputation, reputation, reputation! O, I have lost my reputation! I have lost the immortal part of myself, and what remains is bestial. My reputation, Iago, my reputation!

Iago. As I am an honest man, I had thought you had receiv'd some bodily wound; there is more sense in that than in reputation. Reputation is an idle and most false imposition; oft got without merit, and lost without deserving. You have lost no reputation at all, unless you repute yourself such a loser. What, man! there are more ways to recover the General again; you are but now cast in his mood, a punishment more in policy than in malice; even so as one would beat his offenceless dog to affright an imperious lion. Sue to him again, and he's yours.

Cas. I will rather sue to be despis'd than to deceive so good a commander with so slight, so drunken, and so indiscreet an officer. Drunk! And speak parrot! And squabble, swagger, swear! And discourse fustian with one's own shadow! O thou invisible spirit of wine, if thou hast no name to be known by, let us call thee devil!

Iago. What was he that you follow'd with your sword? What had he done to you?

Cas. I know not.

Iago. Is't possible?

Cas. I remember a mass of things, but nothing distinctly; a quarrel, but nothing wherefore. O God, that men should put an enemy in their mouths to steal away their brains! That we should with joy, pleasance, revel and applause, transform ourselves into beasts!

Iago. Why, but you are now well enough. How come you thus recovered?

Cas. It hath pleas'd the devil drunkenness to give place to the devil wrath. One imperfectness shows me another, to make me frankly despise myself.

Iago. Come, you are too severe a moraller. As the time, the place and the condition of this country stands, I could heartily wish this had not so befall'n; but since it is as it is, mend it for your own good.

Cas. I will ask him for my place again: he shall tell me I am a drunkard. Had I as many mouths as Hydra, such an answer would stop them all. To be now a sensible man, by and by a fool, and presently a beast!

> O strange! Every inordinate cup is unblest, and the
> ingredience is a devil.
>
> *Othello*, II.iii.254-99.

The battle between the higher and lower faculties is of
course a major theme in the tragedies. For example, when
Romeo, distraught at the sentence of banishment which will
separate him from Juliet, tries to commit suicide, Friar
Lawrence urges self-control, warning him that such 'wild acts
denote the unreasonable fury of a beast' (III.iii.110-11). If the
Friar's words of admonition sound harsh, his view of human
nature is nevertheless a more kindly one than that represented
by the official teaching of the Elizabethan Church. Where the
humanist emphasised man's ability to control his passions
through the exercise of reason, Protestant theology stressed
the radical corruption of human nature. In his *The Institution
of Christian Religion* Jean Calvin, greatest and most
influential theologian of the 16th century, attacks the
humanist belief in man's natural dignity.

> Not without cause hath the knowledge of himself
> been in the old Proverb so much commended to man.
> For if it be thought a shame to be ignorant of all
> things that pertain to the course of man's life, then
> much more shameful is the not knowing of ourselves:
> whereby it commeth to pass, that in taking counsel of
> any thing necessary we be miserably dazzled, yea,
> altogether blinded. But how much more profitable
> this lesson is, so much more diligently must we take
> heed, that we do not disorderly use it, as we see some
> of the philosophers have done. For they in exhorting
> man to know himself, do withall appoint this to be the
> end, why he should know himself, that he should not
> be ignorant of his own dignity and excellency, and
> nothing else do they will him to behold in himself, but
> that whereby he may swell with vain confidence, and
> be puffed up with pride. But the knowledge of
> ourselves, first standeth in this point, that considering
> what was given us in creation, and how bountifully
> God continueth His gracious favour toward us, we
> may know how great had been the excellency of our
> nature, if it continued uncorrupted. And we may

withall think upon this, that there is nothing in us of our own, but that we have as it were gotten by borrowing all that God hath bestowed upon us, that we may always hang upon Him. Then, that we call to mind our miserable estate after the fall of Adam, the feeling whereof may throw down all glorying and trust of ourselves, overwhelm us with shame, and truly humble us. For as God at the beginning fashioned us like His own image, to the end to raise up our minds both to the study of virtue and to the meditation of eternal life, so lest the so great nobleness of our kind, which maketh us different from brute beasts, should be drowned with our slothfulness, it is good for us to know that we are therefore endued with reason and understanding, that in keeping a holy and honest life, we should proceed on forward to the appointed end of blessed immortality. But the first dignity cannot come in our mind, but by and by on the other side the heavy sight of our filthiness, and shame doth thrust itself in pretence, since we in the person of the first man are fallen from our first estate, whereupon groweth the hatred and loathing of our selves, and true humility, and there is kindled a new desire to seek for God, in whom every of us may recover those good things, whereof we are found altogether void and empty. . . .

Neither yet am I ignorant how much more pleasant is that other opinion that allureth us rather to consider our good things, than to look upon our miserable neediness and dishonour, which ought to overwhelm us with shame. For there is nothing that man's nature more coveteth, than to be stroked with flattery. And therefore when he heareth the gifts that are in him to be magnified, he leaneth to that side with overmuch lightness of belief, whereby it is so much the less to be marvelled, that herein the greatest part of men have perniciously erred. For since there is naturally planted in all mortal men a more than blind love of themselves, they do most willingly persuade themselves, that there is nothing in them that they ought worthily to hate. So without any maintenance of other, this most vain opinion doth everywhere get credit, that man is abundantly sufficient of himself to make himself live well and blessedly. But if there be any that are content to think more modestly, howsoever they grant somewhat to God, lest they should seem arrogantly to take all to themselves, yet they so part it, that the principal matter of glory and confidence always remaineth with themselves. Now is there some talk, that with her allurements tickleth the pride that already of itself, itcheth within the bones, there is nothing that may more delight them. Therefore as any hath with his extolling most favourably advanced the excellency of man's nature, so hath he been excepted with the well liking rejoicement in manner of all ages. But whatsoever such commendation there be of man's excellence that teaches man to rest in himself, it does nothing but delight with that her sweetness, and indeed so deceives, that it brings to most wretched destruction all them that assent unto it. For to what purpose avails it for us, standing upon all vain confidence to devise, appoint, attempt and go about those things that we think to be for our behalf, and in our first beginning of enterprise to be forsaken and destitute of sound understanding and true strength, and yet to go on boldly till we fall down into destruction? But it cannot otherwise happen to them that have affiance [faith] that they can do any thing by their own power. Therefore if any man give heed to such teachers that hold us in considering only our own good things, he shall not profit in learning to know himself, but shall be carried violently away into the worst kind of ignorance.

Jean Calvin, *The Institution of Christian Religion*
(1535, trans. 1561), fol.58.

Calvin here condemns the humanist belief in man's natural dignity because he believes that the work of grace cannot begin until we have acknowledged our innate depravity. There is little evidence in the plays to suggest that Shakespeare had any real sympathy for the doctrine, fundamental to Protestant theology, of justification by faith alone. However, there is one respect in which he does share Calvin's view of humanity. Of all the tragic heroes there is none who illustrates better the fatal propensity for self-deception described by Calvin than Othello. In his final speech we see what R.B. Heilman has described as 'Shakespeare's sense of the ego's persistent reaching out for the formula that will put the individual in the best possible light' ('Shakespearean Comedy and Tragedy: Implicit Political Analogies', p.31).

> *Oth.* Soft you; a word or two before you go.
> I have done the state some service, and they know't–
> No more of that. I pray you, in your letters,
> When you shall these unlucky deeds relate,
> Speak of me as I am; nothing extenuate,
> Nor set down aught in malice. Then must you speak
> Of one that lov'd not wisely, but too well;
> Of one not easily jealous, but, being wrought,
> Perplexed in the extreme; of one whose hand,
> Like the base Indian, threw a pearl away
> Richer than all his tribe; of one whose subdu'd eyes,
> Albeit unused to the melting mood,
> Drops tears as fast as the Arabian trees
> Their med'cinable gum. Set you down this:
> And say besides that in Aleppo once,
> Where a malignant and a turban'd Turk
> Beat a Venetian and traduc'd the state,
> I took by th' throat the circumcised dog,
> And smote him–thus. [*He stabs himself.*]
> Lod. O bloody period!
> Gra.   All that is spoke is marr'd.
> *Oth.* I kiss'd thee ere I kill'd thee. No way but this–
> Killing my self, to die upon a kiss.
> [*Falls on the bed and dies.*]

Othello, V.ii.341-62.

If Othello shows little awareness in this speech of the limitations of 'honour' as he conceives it, or indeed of the irony of what, in effect, amounts to a comparison of himself to a Turk (the enemy against whom he is supposed to be defending Venetian civilisation), he is certainly not, like Iago, innately evil. A character who declares that he is not 'for love and duty,/But seeming so' (I.i.60-1) owes more to Machiavelli than to Calvin. When Calvin insisted on the depravity of the natural man he did so in order to emphasise his total dependence on divine grace. But Machiavelli had no theological axe to grind. In declaring that mankind is naturally wicked he simply wished to emphasise the need for powerful government.

> According as it is showed by all those that reason of civil government, and so every history is full of examples to that purpose, it is necessary that he who frames a commonwealth, and ordains laws in it, should presuppose that all men are bent to mischief, and that they have a will to put in practice the wickedness of their minds, so oft as occasion shall serve and that when any mischief lies covert for a time, it proceeds from an occasion not known, which is not come to light, because trial of the contrary hath never been made, but time afterwards discovers it, which they say is father of the truth. It seemed that there was in Rome a perfect union of the people and Senate when the Tarquins were banished, and that the nobility having laid by their pride, were become of a popular disposition, and supportable to every one even of the meanest rank. This deceit lay hid, nor was the occasion then known, as long as the Tarquins lived, of whom the nobility being afraid and doubting that upon their ill treating of the people, they might side with them, behaved themselves with good respect towards them. But no sooner were the Tarquins dead, and the nobility delivered of that fear, but they began to spit against the people the poison, that all this while had lurked in their breasts, and in all sorts possible to vex and molest them: which thing confirms what I said before, that men never do good, unless enforced thereto; but where choice is abundant, and liberty at pleasure, confusion and disorder suddenly take place.

Niccolo Machiavelli, *Machiavell's Discourses upon the first Decade of T. Livius* (c.1520, trans. 1636), pp.17-19.

Machiavelli was widely read in 16th-century Europe. But while his importance as a political thinker was undoubtedly recognised by serious writers, including Shakespeare (see Chapter 3), at the same time his name became synonymous in the popular mind with unprincipled villainy. For sheer wanton cruelty there is no character in Renaissance drama to compare with Richard III. In the penultimate scene of the trilogy dealing with the Wars of the Roses we see Richard, as Duke of Gloucester, taking a fierce delight in his own virtuoso performance as torturer and murderer of the saintly King Henry VI.

> *Glo.* Think'st thou I am an executioner?
> *K.Hen.* A persecutor I am sure thou art.
> If murdering innocents be executing,
> Why, then thou art an executioner.
> *Glo.* Thy son I kill'd for his presumption.
> *K.Hen.* Hadst thou been kill'd when first thou didst
>   presume,
> Thou hadst not liv'd to kill a son of mine.
> And thus I prophesy, that many a thousand
> Which now mistrust no parcel of my fear,
> And many an old man's sigh, and many a widow's,
> And many an orphan's water-standing eye–
> Men for their sons, wives for their husbands,
> Orphans for their parents' timeless death–
> Shall rue the hour that ever thou wast born.

> * * *

> *Glo.* I'll hear no more. Die, prophet, in thy speech.
> [*Stabs him*].
> For this, amongst the rest, was I ordain'd.
> *K.Hen.* Ay, and for much more slaughter after this.
> O, God forgive my sins and pardon thee! [*Dies*].
> *Glo.* What, will the aspiring blood of Lancaster
> Sink in the ground? I thought it would have mounted.
> See how my sword weeps for the poor King's death.
> O, may such purple tears be alway shed
> From those that wish the downfall of our house!
> If any spark of life be yet remaining,

> Down, down to hell; and say I sent thee, thither–
> [*Stabs him again.*]
> I, that have neither pity, love, nor fear.
> Indeed, 'tis true that Henry told me of;
> For I have often heard my mother say
> I came into the world with my legs forward.
> Had I not reason, think ye, to make haste
> And seek their ruin that usurp'd our right?
> The midwife wonder'd; and the women cried
> 'O, Jesus bless us, he is born with teeth!'
> And so I was, which plainly signified
> That I should snarl, and bite, and play the dog.
> Then, since the heavens have shap'd my body so,
> Let hell make crook'd my mind to answer it.
> I have no brother, I am like no brother;
> And this word 'love', which greybeards call divine,
> Be resident in men like one another,
> And not in me! I am myself alone.
> Clarence, beware; thou keep'st me from the light,
> But I will sort a pitchy day for thee;
> For I will buzz abroad such prophesies
> That Edward shall be fearful of his life;
> And then to purge his fear, I'll be thy death.
> King Henry and the Prince his son are gone.
> Clarence, thy turn is next, and then the rest;
> Counting myself but bad till I be best.
> I'll throw thy body in another room,
> And triumph, Henry, in thy day of doom.
> [*Exit with the body.*]

3 Henry VI, V.vi.30-43; 57-93.

By asserting the innate evil in human nature, Protestant theology on the one hand and Machiavellian empiricism on the other had the effect of undermining the traditional Christian humanist emphasis on man's dignity and rationality. Radical as these influences were, however, they represented a less serious threat to traditional views of human nature than the sort of primitivist arguments put forward by Starkey's Reginald Pole. For the corollary of the primitivist belief in man's natural innocence and its concomitant suspicion of reason was a distrust of all authority.

With the discovery of the Americas and the Caribbean in the 15th and 16th centuries the possibility began to suggest itself that the legendary Golden Age was not just a poetic fiction or even a historical period of remote antiquity, but a contemporary reality. Just as the great voyages of discovery to the South Pacific in the 1760s reawakened European interest in the idea of the noble savage, so 16th-century travellers' reports caught the popular imagination with their idealised accounts of the New World. A frequently repeated theme in these reports is the comparison between the newly discovered primitive societies and traditional poetic accounts of the Golden Age. In one of his most famous essays Montaigne uses a traveller's description of the lives of Brazilian Indians as an opportunity to turn conventional arguments about art and nature upside down.

> I find (as far as I have been informed) there is nothing in that nation, that is either barbarous or savage, unless men call that barbarism, which is not common to them. As indeed, we have no other aim of truth and reason, than the example and idea of the opinions and customs of the country we live in. Then there is ever perfect religion, perfect policy, perfect and complete use of all things. They are even savage, as we call those fruits wild, which nature of herself, and of her ordinary progress hath produced; whereas indeed, they are those which ourselves have altered by our artifical devices, and diverted from their common order, we should rather term savage. In those are the true and most profitable virtues, and natural proprieties most lively and vigorous, which in these we have bastardized, applying them to the pleasure of our corrupted taste. And if notwithstanding in divers fruits of those countries that were never tilled, we shall find, that in respect of ours they are most excellent, and as delicate unto our taste, there is no reason, art should gain the point of honour of our great and puissant mother nature. We have so much by inventions, surcharged the beauties and riches of her works, that we have altogether over-choked her; yet wherever her purity shineth, she makes our vain,

and frivolous enterprises wonderfully ashamed.

All our endeavours or wit cannot so much as reach to represent the nest of the least birdlet, its contexture, beauty, profit and use, no nor the web of a silly [simple] spider. All things (saith Plato) are produced, either by nature, by fortune, or by art. The greatest and fairest by one or other of the first two, the least and imperfect by the last. Those nations seem therefore so barbarous unto me, because they have received very little fashion from human wit, and are yet near their original naturality. The laws of nature do yet command them, which are but little bastardized by ours. And that with such purity, as I am sometimes grieved the knowledge of it came no sooner to light, at what time there were men that better than we could have judged of it. I am sorry Licurgus and Plato had it not, for me seemeth that what in those nations we see by experience, doth not only exceed all the pictures wherewith licentious poesy hath proudly embellished the golden age, and all her quaint inventions to feign a happy condition of man, but also the conception and desire of philosophy. They could not imagine a genuity so pure and simple, as we see it by experience; nor ever believe our society might be maintained with so little art and human combination. It is a nation, would I answer Plato, that hath no kind of traffic [trade], no knowledge of letters, no intelligence of numbers, no name of magistrate, nor of politic superiority; no use of service, of riches, or of poverty; no contracts, no successions, no dividences [social divisions], no occupation but idle; no respect of kindred, but common, no apparel but natural, no manuring of lands, no use of wine, corn, or metal. The very words that import lying, falsehood, treason, dissimulation, covetousness, envy, detraction, and pardon, were never heard of amongst them. How dissonant would he [Plato] find his imaginary commonwealth from this perfection?

Michel de Montaigne, 'Of the Cannibals',
The Essays (1588, trans. 1603), pp.101-2.

Montaigne's account of South America is essentially the product of a literary imagination: he is seeing the Indian through Ovid's eyes and comparing what he has heard at second-hand of primitive Brazilian society with poetic accounts of the Golden Age. The fact that Gonzalo uses the same phrases in describing his imaginary commonwealth in *The Tempest* must raise the question of whether Shakespeare shares Montaigne's view of human nature. That primitivist arguments like Montaigne's were seen as a threat to established authority is clear from the reaction of a writer like Thomas Cooper in an anti-Marprelate tract of 1589.

> At the beginning (say they) when God had first made the world, all men were alike, there was no principality, there was no bondage, or villeinage: that grew afterwards by violence and cruelty. Therefore why should we live in this miserable slavery under these proud lords and crafty lawyers? etc. Wherefore it behoveth all faithful Christians and wise governors, to beware of this false and crafty policy. If this argument pass now, and be allowed as good at this time against the ecclesiastical state, it may be, you shall hereinafter by other instruments than yet are stirring hear the same reason applied to other states also, which yet seem not to be touched, and therefore can be content to wink at this dealing toward bishops and preachers. But when the next house is on fire, a wise man will take heed, least the sparks thereof fall into his own.

> Thomas Cooper, *An Admonition to the People of England* (1589), pp.118-9.

But Cooper's emotive condemnation of the primitivist argument would be unlikely to persuade someone who did not already share his conservative political views. A more carefully reasoned case is put by Starkey in a passage from his *Dialogue* where Pole and Lupset, now in agreement on essential points, discuss the futility of utopian social dreams.

Pole. The wise philosopher Plato in all his common-

wealth chiefly laboured to see good officers, heads
and rulers, the which should be, as it were, lively
laws; for the which cause also, after mine opinion, he
thought nothing necessary to write any laws to his
commonalty; for if the heads in a commonwealth
were both just, good and wise, there should need
none other laws to the people. But how might this be
brought to pass, Master Lupset, in our commonwealth and country? Think you it were possible?

Lupset. I think by no man's wit. And therefore Plato
imagined only and dreamed upon such a commonwealth as never yet was found, nor never, I think,
shall be, except God would send down His angels and
of them make a city; for man by nature is so frail and
corrupt, that so many wise men in a commonalty to
find, I think it plain impossible.

Pole. Well, Master Lupset, here you must understand
that we look not for such heads as Plato describeth in
his policy, for that is out of hope with us to be found,
nor yet for such wise men as the Stoics describe, and
ancient philosophers. But after a more civil and
common sort we will measure the wisdom of them
whom we would to rule – that is to say, such as will
not in all things neither follow their own affections,
neither yet in whom all affects are drowned and taken
quite away, but, observing a certain reasonable mean,
ever have their eyes fixed to the commonwealth, and
that above all thing ever to prefer, to that ever redress
all their acts, thoughts and deeds. Such men, I say, if
we might set in our commonwealth and policy,
should be sufficient for us.

Lupset. Sir, I think we were happy if we might such
find.

Pole. Well, let us consider then, and proceed. First,
this is certain in our commonwealth as it is instituted:
a great part of this matter hangeth upon one pin; for
this is sure – our country is not so barren of honest
men but such might be found, specially if the youth
were a little brought up after such manner as we shall
touch hereafter. The pin that I speak of is this: to have
a good prince to govern and rule. This is the ground

of all felicity in the civil life. This is foundation of all good policy in such a kind of state as is in our country. The prince institutes and makes almost all under-officers; he has authority and rule of all. Therefore, if we could find a mean to have a good prince commonly, this should be a common remedy almost, as I said, for all the rest of the misorders in the policy.

Thomas Starkey, *Dialogue Between Reginald Pole and Thomas Lupset,* pp.150-1.

Pole and Lupset agree that, desirable as it would be to dispense with laws altogether, it is unrealistic, given the facts of human nature, to imagine that such a society could ever survive. The same point is made in dramatic terms in *The Tempest* as we see Gonzalo's dream of an egalitarian utopia punctured by the sardonic interruptions of Antonio and Sebastian.

Shakespeare was clearly aware of the appeal of the primitivist view of human nature. But he had enough of the realist in him to recognise, like Machiavelli, that in an imperfect world where men like Antonio and Sebastian exist, there is an overwhelming need for powerful government. What form that government should take and what limitations should be placed on its authority are the political questions which were of most vital concern to the 16th century.

2 Forms of Government

The ten-year period during which Shakespeare wrote most of his historical and political plays was marked by an unprecedented interest in constitutional questions. From the time of the English Reformation of 1533-34 writers had expressed reservations about the new powers which Henrician, and later Elizabethan pamphleteers claimed for the crown. But it was not until the 1590s, when England was no longer threatened with invasion by a foreign power, that criticism of the Tudor doctrine of absolute obedience to royal authority became widespread. When dissident pamphleteers, both Catholic and Puritan, challenged this propaganda, the Elizabethan establishment responded by appealing to a principle of order which was enshrined in the laws of nature itself. Ulysses' long speech on degree in the first act of *Troilus and Cressida* contains a classic statement of these arguments. But Ulysses' words should not be taken out of their dramatic context; in particular we should not assume that 'Ulysses . . . completely expresses his creator's views' (A.L. Rowse, *William Shakespeare: A Biography* p.342). *Troilus and Cressida* is a story of love's betrayal set against the background of a futile war waged by proud and childish men whose analytic powers have outstripped their common sense. Portia's words in *The Merchant of Venice* – 'The brain may devise laws for the blood, but a hot temper leaps o'er a cold decree' (I.ii.14-15) – apply with equal truth to both Greek and Trojan generals. Ulysses is no exception. His pride injured by the mocking taunts of Achilles, the Greek commander, delivers the following diagnosis of his army's problems.

> The heavens themselves, the planets, and this centre,
> Observe degree, priority, and place,
> Insisture, course, proportion, season, form,
> Office, and custom, in all line of order;
> And therefore is the glorious planet Sol
> In noble eminence enthron'd and spher'd

Amidst the other, whose med'cinable eye
Corrects the ill aspects of planets evil,
And posts, like the commandment of a king,
Sans check, to good and bad. But when the planets
In evil mixture to disorder wander,
What plagues and what portents, what mutiny,
What raging of the sea, shaking of earth,
Commotion in the winds! Frights, changes, horrors,
Divert and crack, rend and deracinate,
The unity and married calm of states
Quite from their fixture! O, when degree is shak'd,
Which is the ladder of all high designs,
The enterprise is sick! How could communities,
Degrees in schools, and brotherhoods in cities,
Peaceful commerce from dividable shores,
The primogenity and due of birth,
Prerogative of age, crowns, sceptres, laurels,
But by degree, stand in authentic place?
Take but degree away, untune that string,
And hark what discord follows! Each thing melts
In mere oppugnancy: the bounded waters
Should lift their bosoms higher than the shores,
And make a sop of all this solid globe;
Strength should be lord of imbecility.
And the rude son should strike his father dead;
Force should be right; or, rather, right and wrong—
Between whose endless jar justice resides—
Should lose their names, and so should justice too.
Then everything includes itself in power,
Power into will, will into appetite;
And appetite, an universal wolf,
So doubly seconded with will and power,
Must make perforce an universal prey,
And last eat up himself.

Troilus and Cressida, I.iii.85–124.

Removed from their ironic context, these well-known lines have often been taken as a poetic summary of Shakespeare's own political views. 'There can be no doubt,' writes one critic, 'that Shakespeare believed in this almost universally-accepted concept of degree, and that he accepted the Tudor doctrines of absolutism and passive obedience' (I. Ribner, *The English History Play in the Age of Shakespeare*, p.154). Such views were undoubtedly held by many Elizabethans but they represent only one end of a wide spectrum of political theories.

The Elizabethan doctrine of order and obedience described by Tillyard and other critics is an amalgam of medieval and Reformation ideas. In the Middle Ages society was seen as a community of individuals united by the common purpose of living virtuously in accordance with God's commands. In the 13th century St Thomas Aquinas explained that just as the universe was ruled by a wise and rational providence, so it followed by analogy that the various degrees of society should be governed by the reason of one man (*On Kingship*, pp.53-4). These ideas are summed up in Sir Thomas Elyot's *The Governour*, one of the most widely-read humanist texts of the 16th century.

A public weal [state] is a body living, compact or made of sundry estates and degrees of men, which is disposed by the order of equity and governed by the rule and moderation of reason. . . . [But] take away order from all things what should then remain? Certes nothing finally, except some man would imagine eftsoons chaos: which of some is expounded a confused mixture. Also where there is any lack of order needs must be perpetual conflict . . . .

But now to prove, by example of those things that be within the compass of man's knowledge, of which estimation order is, not only among men but also with God, albeit His wisdom, bounty and magnificence can be with no tongue or pen sufficiently expressed. Hath not He set degrees and estates in all His glorious works? . . . Behold the four elements whereof the body of man is compact, how they be set in their places called spheres, higher or lower, according to the sovereignty of their natures, that is to say, the fire as the most pure element, having in it nothing that is corruptible, in his place is highest and above other elements. The air, which next to the fire is most pure in substance, is in the second sphere or place. The water, which is somewhat consolidate, and approacheth to corruption, is next unto the earth. The earth, which is of substance gross and ponderous, is set of all elements most lowest.

Behold also the order that God hath put generally in all His creatures, beginning at the most inferior or base, and ascending upward; He made not only herbs to garnish the earth, but also trees of a more eminent stature than herbs, and yet in the one and the other be degrees of qualities, some pleasant to behold, some delicate or good in taste, others wholesome and medicinable, some commodious and necessary. Semblably in birds, beasts, and fishes, some be good for the sustenance of man, some bear things profitable to sundry uses, others be apt to occupation and labour; in diverse is strength and fierceness only; in many is both strength and commodity; some others serve for pleasure; none of them hath all these qualities; few have the more part or many, specially beauty, strength, and profit. But where any is found that hath many of the said properties, he is more set by than all the others, and by that estimation the order of his place and degree evidently appeareth; so that every kind of trees, herbs, birds, beasts, and fishes, beside their diversity of forms, have (as who saith) a peculiar disposition appropered unto them by God their creator, so that in every thing is order, and without order may be nothing stable or permanent; and it may not be called order, except it do contain in it degrees, high and base, according to the merit or estimation of the thing that is ordered.

Now to return to the estate of mankind, for whose use all the said creatures were ordained of God, and also excelleth them all by prerogative of knowledge and wisdom, it seemeth that in him should be no less providence of God declared than in the inferior creatures; but rather with a more perfect order and disposition. And therefore it appeareth that God giveth not to every man like gifts of grace, or of nature, but to some more, some less, as it liketh His divine majesty . . . .

Notwithstanding forasmuch as understanding is the most excellent gift that man can receive in his creation, whereby he doth approach most nigh unto the similitude of God, which understanding is the principal part of the soul, it is therefore congruent and according that as one excelleth another in that influence, as thereby being next to the similitude of his maker, so should the estate of his person be advanced in degree or place where understanding may profit, which is also distributed into sundry uses, faculties, and offices, necessary for the living and governance of mankind. And like as the angels which be most fervent in contemplation be highest exalted in glory, (after the opinion of holy doctors), and also the fire which is the most pure of elements, and also doth clarify the other inferior elements, is deputed to the highest sphere or place: so in this world, they which excel other in this influence of understanding, and do employ it to the detaining of other within the bounds of reason, and show them how to provide for their necessary living; such ought to be set in a more high place than the residue where they may see and also be seen, that by the beams of their excellent wit, showed through the glass of authority, other of inferior understanding may be directed to the way of virtue and commodious living . . . . Wherefore undoubtedly the best and most sure governance is by one king or prince, which ruleth only for the weal of his people to him subject; and that manner of governance is best approved, and hath longest continued, and is most ancient. For who can deny but that all things in heaven and earth is governed by one God, by one perpetual order, by one providence? One sun ruleth over the day, and one moon over the night, and to descend down to the earth, in a little beast, which of all others is most to be marvelled at, I mean the bee, is left to man by nature, as it seemeth, a perpetual figure of a just governance or rule, who hath among them one principal bee for their governor, who excelleth all other in greatness.

Sir Thomas Elyot, *The Boke Named The Governour*
(1531), pp.1-9.

Fundamental to Elyot's view of society is the notion of the state as 'a body living compact or made of sundry estates and degrees of men'. The body/state analogy is an ancient one; it is the natural expression of a theory of cosmos which believed that the organising principle of degree was repeated on every plane of existence. The opening scene of *Coriolanus* is based on this traditional analogy. The words of the First Citizen make it clear that the context of this exchange between a Roman patrician and a group of plebeians is a state of famine in which the populace is accusing its rulers of bad faith. It is ominous that in this situation Menenius should identify the senators of Rome, not with the 'kingly crowned head' – seat of reason – but with a 'taunting' belly. In this perversion of traditional wisdom lie, in part, the seeds of the discord which the play unfolds.

> *1 Cit.* Care for us! True, indeed! They ne'er car'd for us yet. Suffer us to famish, and their storehouses cramm'd with grain; make edicts for usury, to support usurers; repeal daily any wholesome act established against the rich, and provide more piercing statutes daily to chain up and restrain the poor. If the wars eat us not up, they will; and there's all the love they bear us.
> *Men.* Either you must
> Confess yourselves, wondrous malicious,
> Or be accus'd of folly. I shall tell you
> A pretty tale. It may be you have heard it;
> But, since it serves my purpose, I will venture
> To stale't a little more.
> *1 Cit.* Well, I'll hear it, sir; yet you must not think to fob off our disgrace with a tale. But, an't please you, deliver.
> *Men.* There was a time when all the body's members
> Rebell'd against the belly; thus accus'd it:
> That only like a gulf it did remain

I' th' midst o' th' body, idle and unactive,
Still cupboarding the viand, never bearing
Like labour with the rest; where th' other instruments
Did see and hear, devise, instruct, walk, feel,
And, mutually participate, did minister
Unto the appetite and affection common
Of the whole body. The belly answer'd—
1 *Cit.* Well, sir, what answer made the belly?
Men. Sir, I shall tell you. With a kind of smile,
Which ne'er came from the lungs, but even thus—
For look you, I may make the belly smile
As well as speak—it tauntingly replied
To th' discontented members, the mutinous parts
That envied his receipt; even so fitly
As you malign our senators for that
They are not such as you.
1 *Cit.*   Your belly's answer—What?
The kingly crowned head, the vigilant eye,
The counsellor heart, the arm our soldier,
Our steed the leg, the tongue our trumpeter,
With other muniments and petty helps
Is this our fabric, if that they—
Men.   What then?
Fore me, this fellow speaks! What then? What then?
1 *Cit.* Should by the cormorant belly be restrain'd,
Who is the sink o' th' body—
Men.   Well, what then?
1 *Cit.* The former agents, if they did complain,
What could the belly answer?
Men.   I will tell you;
If you'll bestow a small—of what you have little—
Patience awhile, you'st hear the belly's answer.
1 *Cit.* Y'are long about it.
Men.   Note me this, good friend:
Your most grave belly was deliberate,
Not rash like his accusers, and thus answered.
'True is it, my incorporate friends,' quoth he
'That I receive the general food at first
Which you do live upon; and fit it is,
Because I am the storehouse and the shop
Of the whole body. But, if you do remember,

I send it through the rivers of your blood,
Even to the court, the heart, to th' seat o' th' brain;
And, through the cranks and offices of man,
The strongest nerves and small inferior veins
From me receive that natural competency
Whereby they live. And though that all at once
You, my good friends'—this says the belly; mark me.
1 *Cit.* Ay, sir; well, well.
Men.   'Though all at once cannot
See what I do deliver out to each,
Yet I can make my audit up, that all
From me do back receive the flour of all,
And leave me but the bran.' What say you to't?
1 *Cit.* It was an answer. How apply you this?
Men. The senators of Rome are this good belly,
And you the mutinous members; for, examine
Their counsels and their cares, digest things rightly
Touching the weal o' th' common, you shall find
No public benefit which you receive
But it proceeds or comes from them to you,
And no way from yourselves. What do you think,
You, the great toe of this assembly?
1 *Cit.* I the great toe? Why the great toe?
Men. For that, being one o' th' lowest, basest, poorest,
Of this most wise rebellion, thou goest foremost.
Thou rascal, that art worst in blood to run,
Lead'st first to win some vantage.
But make you ready your stiff bats and clubs.
Rome and her rats are at the point of battle;
The one side must have bale.

                              Coriolanus, I.i.77-161.

The body/state analogy so widely used by Elizabethan political writers expresses an organicist view of society which is essentially medieval. Quite alien to the Middle Ages, however, was the doctrine of absolute obedience which often accompanied this theory. Medieval writers emphasise that kingship is an office which is held in trust. Although his subjects owe him allegiance, a ruler's right to demand obedience is dependent on his deserving it. A summary of these medieval commonplaces may be found in the late 14th-century poem *Confessio Amantis* (VII.3067-3083) by John Gower, whom Shakespeare honoured by giving his name to the chorus in *Pericles*.

With the Reformation there emerged a new conception of sovereignty in which the crown claimed far greater powers than it had previously enjoyed. The revolution of 1533-34 had been carried out with the full cooperation of parliament, and the new monarchy was in fact subject to strict constitutional limits. It was the need to counter not only domestic dissatisfaction but also the very real threat of retaliatory invasion from Catholic Europe that led to the promulgation of a doctrine of kingship which stressed the sacrosanctity of the crown and emphasised the paramount duty of obedience. The cult of quasi-divine sovereignty which marked the latter years of Elizabeth's reign, illustrated in this extract from a pro-monarchist pamphlet, has its origins in the Henrician Reformation.

> It followeth that we speak of the manner of estate of this most royal monarchy and best kind of kingdom, that is, how, and in what case it standeth, as touching the power, and authority appertaining thereunto. For it is not sufficient that so royal a prince be descended lineally, and lawfully into his kingdom, but he must also possess, and exercise such royal and princely power therein, as is most fit for his worthiness and for his subject's happiness. Neither in so extreme manner, as to make a god of himself, as Alexander the Great would have done, and slaves of his vassals, as the Great Turk at this day doth, neither yet in so slender sort, as to have the sword carried after him, as the Duke of Venice hath, and to be but a little better, than a cipher, or shadow of a prince.
>
> He is for to have therefore, by the grace and permission of Almighty God, that power which the Greeks call *arkan exousian* [supreme authority]; the Latins *maiestatem;* the Italians *signoria;* the French-men *souveraineté:* that is, power full and perpetual over all his subjects in general, and over every one in

particular. Not to rule for a year only, as the consuls of Rome did; nor for two years, as the dukes of Genoa do; nor for three, as the viceroys of Naples; nor for nine, or ten years, as the great Archon of Athens did; not to be dictator for a day only, as Mamercus was; nor for eight days, as Servilus Priscus; or for fifteen, as Cincinnatus; no not yet for fifteen years, as Sulla had gotten it granted unto him by a law to be dictator fourscore years (although he reigned but four) and then after the term of years expired, to render up his government unto another, perhaps unto a stranger, perhaps unto his enemy. But his power shall last, by God's grace, perpetually: first during his own life in himself, and then after his death in his sons and successors.

Neither is he countable of such his government, saving to God, and his conscience, else not unto any other; in such short, as legates, lieutenants, presidents, regents, etc. are, who though they have authority sometimes during their lives, yet are they to render account unto those which gave them the same. The Doges of Venice, if they govern not well, are deposed by the Signory of the gentlemen: as Teodatus, and Galla of Malomocco were banished, and had their eyes put out, because they ruled too lordly. The governors of Bologna la Grassa, when they go out of their office, are bound to render account unto two Syndici. The dictators of Rome were forced by the tribunes to render reason unto the people. The regents of Scotland, the Lords Protectors of England, although they rule never so highly during the minority of their princes, yet we see that after they are out of their offices, they are constrained to answer unto many oppositions . . . . Our prince therefore is not to receive his power from any except from God the giver of all power. For if he receive it from any other higher prince, then is he not the principal, and supreme magistrate, but there is an other higher, and greater than he. For as honour dependeth more of the giver, than of the receiver, so likewise that power is greatest, from whence the others are derived. But our prince, who is the image of God on earth, and as it were *un minor essempio* [a pattern in little] of His almighty power, is not to acknowledge any greater than himself, nor any authority greater than his own. Wherefore as he is not to receive his power from any, so is he neither to be subject unto any higher power, either at home, or abroad, though some do maintain that a prince ought to be subject unto the states and peers of his realm, as the kings of Lacedemon were to the Ephorian opinion, if it be not well tempered, and conveniently limited, most prejudicial unto the state of a monarchy, perverting and converting the same into a mere aristocracy. Much less is he subject in anything unto the multitude of the common people, who as they have more authority are for the most part more insolent, and more disposed unto rebellion. Wherefore in all well ordained kingdoms these have no other than a voice supplicative, those a voice deliberative, and the prince only a voice definitive.

> Charles Merbury, *A Brief Discourse of Royal Monarchy as of the Best Commonweal*, (1581), pp.40-4.

Merbury's arguments in defence of absolute monarchy are frequently repeated by Elizabethan pamphleteers. It is a theme which is dear to the heart of Shakespeare's Richard II. When the Duke of Aumerle warns Richard of the threat posed by the rebellious nobles who have united under the aggrieved Bolingbroke, the king appeals to the sacrosanctity of his office.

> *Aum.* My lord . . . we are too remiss;
> Whilst Bolingbroke, through our security,
> Grows strong and great in substance and in power.
> *K.Rich.* Discomfortable cousin! know'st thou not
> That when the searching eye of heaven is hid,
> Behind the globe, that lights the lower world,
> Then thieves and robbers range abroad unseen
> In murders and in outrage boldly here;
> But when from under this terrestrial ball
> He fires the proud tops of the eastern pines

And darts his light through every guilty hole,
Then murders, treasons, and detested sins,
The cloak of night being pluck'd from off their backs,
Stand bare and naked, trembling at themselves?
So when this thief, this traitor, Bolingbroke,
Who all this while hath revell'd in the night,
Whilst we were wand'ring with the Antipodes,
Shall see us rising in our throne, the east,
His treasons will sit blushing in his face,
Not able to endure the sight of day,
But self-affrighted tremble at his sin.
Not all the water in the rough rude sea
Can wash the balm off from an anointed king;
The breath of worldly men cannot depose
The deputy elected by the Lord.
For every man that Bolingbroke hath press'd
To lift shrewd steel against our golden crown,
God for his Richard hath in heavenly pay
A glorious angel. Then, if angels fight,
Weak men must fall; for heaven still guards the right.

Richard II, III.ii.33-62.

Richard's words are of course an anachronism. Such absolute views of kingship were not formulated in England until Henry's act of rebellion against papal authority made them necessary. In his dramatisation of pre-Reformation history Shakespeare is reflecting the political preoccupations of his own time. But if Richard's view reflects a large body of Elizabethan opinion, it is not the only contemporary view of kingship. From the safety of the continent the Catholic polemicist Robert Parsons proposed radical limitations on royal power.

A king or prince is a man as others be, and thereby not only subject to errors in judgement, but also, to passionate affections in his will. For this cause, it was necessary that the commonwealth, as it gave him this great power over them, so it should assign him also the best helps that might be, for directing and rectifying both his will and judgement, and make him therein as like in government to God, whom he representeth, as man's frailty can reach unto.

For this consideration they assigned to him first of all the assistance and direction of law, whereby to govern, which law is a certain mind disquieted with no disordinate affection, as men's minds commonly be. For that when a law is made, for the most part, it is made upon the consideration and deliberation, and without perturbation of evil affections, as anger, envy, hatred, rashness, or the like passions, and it is referred to some good end and commodity of the commonwealth; which law being once made, remaineth so still without alteration or partial affection, being indifferent to all and partial to none, but telleth one tale to every man. And in this it resembleth the perfection as it were of God Himself, for the which cause [Aristotle] . . . addeth a notable wise saying, to wit, that 'he which joineth a law to govern with the prince joineth God to the prince, but he that joineth to the prince his affection to govern, joineth a beast'. For that men's affections and concupiscences are common also to beasts, so that a prince ruling by law is more than a man, or a man deified, and a prince ruling by affections, is less than a man, or a man brutified. In another place also the same philosopher saith that a prince that leaveth law and ruleth himself and others by his own appetite and affections, 'of all creatures is the worst and of all beasts is the most furious and dangerous', for that nothing is so outragious as injustice armed, and no armour is so strong as wit and authority, whereof the first he hath in that he is a man, and the other in that he is a prince.

For this cause then all commonwealths have prescribed laws unto their princes, to govern thereby, as by a most excellent certain and immutable rule. . . . My opinion in this behalf is far . . . from the abject and wicked flattery of such as affirm princes, to be subject to no law or limitation at all, either in authority government, life or succession, but as though by nature they had been created kings from the beginning of the world, or as though the commonwealth had been made for them and not they for the commonwealth, or as though they had begotten or purchased or given life to the weal public, and not that the weal public had exalted them or given them their authority, honour and dignity. So these flatterers do free them from all obligation, duty, reverence or respect unto the whole body whereof they are the heads; nay expressly they say and affirm that 'all men's goods, bodies and lives, are the prince's at their pleasures to dispose of; that they are under no law or account-giving whatsoever; that they succeed by nature and generation only, and not by any authority admission or approbation of the commonwealth; and that consequently no merit or demerit of their persons is to be respected, nor any considerations of their natures or qualities, to wit of capacity, disposition or other personal circumstances is to be had or admitted, and, do they what they list, no authority is there under God to chasten them'.

All these absurd paradoxes, have some men of our days uttered in flattery of princes.

> Robert Parsons, *A Conference About the Next Succession to the Crown of England* (1594), pp.21-2; 35-6.

Parsons' fears concerning the wisdom of vesting absolute power in a king are shared by the conspirators in *Julius Caesar*. If the course of action which Brutus proposes in the first line of his soliloquy at the beginning of Act II seems a desperate one, he makes it clear in line three that his motive is not personal advancement, but the welfare of the state.

> It must be by his death; and for my part,
> I know no personal cause to spurn at him,
> But for the general: he would be crown'd.
> How that might change his nature, there's the
>   question.
> It is the bright day that brings forth the adder,
> And that craves wary walking. Crown him –that!
> And then, I grant, we put a sting in him
> That at his will he may do danger with.
> Th' abuse of greatness is, when it disjoins

Remorse from power; and to speak truth of Caesar,
I have not known when his affections sway'd
More than his reason. But 'tis a common proof
That lowliness is young ambition's ladder,
Whereto the climber-upward turns his face;
But when he once attains the upmost round,
He then unto the ladder turns his back,
Looks in the clouds, scorning the base degrees
By which he did ascend. So Caesar may.
Then, lest he may, prevent. And since the quarrel
Will bear no colour for the thing he is,
Fashion it thus–that what he is, augmented,
Would run to these and these extremities;
And therefore think him as a serpent's egg,
Which, hatch'd, would as his kind grow mischievous,
And kill him in the shell.

Julius Caesar, II.i.10-34.

It is sometimes argued that the theme of *Julius Caesar* is the tragic failure of a republican movement to purge Rome of tyranny. Dangerous as Caesar's autocratic style of government may seem to the honest Brutus, however, the events of the play appear to undermine the fundamental premise of the republican case for representative government. Assassinating Caesar in the name of 'Liberty, freedom, and enfranchisement' (III.i.81), the conspirators quickly discover that they have merely unleashed a new form of tyranny, that of the mob. After the plebeians have dispersed with Mark Antony's rhetoric of vengeance ringing in their ears (III.ii), there follows a short scene of farcical brutality. In the shockingly pointless murder of the harmless Cinna is symbolised the inveterate irrationality of the mob.

Cin. I dreamt to-night that I did feast with Caesar,
And things unluckily charge my fantasy.
I have no will to wander forth of doors,
Yet something leads me forth.
1 *Pleb.* What is your name?
2 *Pleb.* Whither are you going?
3 *Pleb.* Where do you dwell?
4 *Pleb.* Are you a married man or a bachelor?

2 *Pleb.* Answer every man directly.
1 *Pleb.* Ay, and briefly.
4 *Pleb.* Ay, and wisely.
3 *Pleb.* Ay, and truly, you were best.
Cin. What is my name? Whither am I going? Where
do I dwell? Am I a married man or a bachelor? Then
to answer every man directly and briefly, wisely and
truly: wisely, I say I am a bachelor.
2 *Pleb.* That's as much as to say they are fools that
marry. You'll bear me a bang for that, I fear. Proceed
directly.
Cin. Directly, I am going to Caesar's funeral.
1 *Pleb.* As a friend or an enemy?
Cin. As a friend.
2 *Pleb.* That matter is answered directly.
4 *Pleb.* For your dwelling–briefly.
Cin. Briefly, I dwell by the Capitol.
3 *Pleb.* Your name, sir, truly.
Cin. Truly, my name is Cinna.
1 *Pleb.* Tear him to pieces; he's a conspirator!
Cin. I am Cinna the poet, I am Cinna the poet.
4 *Pleb.* Tear him for his bad verses, tear him for his
bad verses!
Cin. I am not Cinna the conspirator.
4 *Pleb.* It is no matter, his name's Cinna; pluck but
his name out of his heart, and turn him going.
3 *Pleb.* Tear him, tear him! Come, brands, ho!
fire-brands! To Brutus', to Cassius'! Burn all! Some
to Decius' house, and some to Casca's; some to
Ligarius'. Away, go!

Julius Caesar, III.iii.1-38.

The irrationality of the mob is a topic which many of
Shakespeare's aristocratic characters are fond of rehearsing,
none more so than Coriolanus. But there is an important
difference between hatred of the mob and an impartial
recognition of its limitations. More telling than Coriolanus'
irresponsibly passionate tirades against the plebeians (for
example I.i.165-86) is what they reveal of themselves.

1 *Cit.* Once, if he do require our voices, we ought not

to deny him.

2 *Cit.* We may, sir, if we will.

3 *Cit.* We have power in ourselves to do it, but it is a
power that we have no power to do; for if he show
us his wounds and tell us his deeds, we are to put
our tongues into those wounds and speak for them;
so, if he tell us his noble deeds, we must also tell
him our noble acceptance of them. Ingratitude is
monstrous, and for the multitude to be ingrateful
were to make a monster of the multitude; of the
which we being members should bring ourselves to
be monstrous members.

1 *Cit.* And to make us no better thought of, a little
help will serve; for once we stood up about the
corn, he himself stuck not to call us the many-
headed multitude.

3 *Cit.* We have been call'd so of many; not that our
heads are some brown, some black, some abram,
some bald, but that our wits are so diversely
colour'd; and truly I think if all our wits were to
issue out of one skull, they would fly east, west,
north, south, and their consent of one direct way
should be at once to all the points o' th' compass.

2 *Cit.* Think you so? Which way do you judge my
wit would fly?

3 *Cit.* Nay, your wit will not so soon out as another
man's will—'tis strongly wedg'd up in a block-head;
but if it were at liberty 'twould sure southward.

2 *Cit.* Why that way?

3 *Cit.* To lose itself in a fog; where being three parts
melted away with rotten dews, the fourth would
return for conscience' sake, to help to get thee a
wife.

Coriolanus, II.iii.1-33.

Behind this view of the common people as fickle, indecisive
and politically irresponsible lies a long tradition of
anti-populist satire. The following example from a contemporary French writer was translated into English shortly
before Shakespeare wrote *Coriolanus*.

The people (we understand here the vulgar sort, the

popular rout, a kind of people under what covert soever of base, servile, and mechanical condition) are a strange beast with many heads, and which in few words cannot [but] be described inconstant and variable, without stay, like the waves of the sea: they are moved and appeased, they allow and disallow one and the same thing at one and the same instant; there is nothing more easy than to drive them into what passion he will; they love not wars for the true end thereof, nor peace for rest and quietness, but for variety's sake, and the change that there is from the one to the other; confusion makes them desire order, and when they have it, they like it not; they run always one contrary to another, and there is no time pleaseth but what is to come.

They are light to believe, to gather together news, especially such as are most hurtful, holding all reports for assured truths. With a whistle, or some sonnet of news, a man may assemble them together like bees at the sound of a basin.

Without judgement, reason, discretion. Their judgement and wisdom is but by chance, like a cast at dice, unadvised and headlong of all things, and always ruled by opinion or custom, or the greater number, going all in a line, like sheep that run after those that go before them, and not by reason and truth.

Envious and malicious, enemies to good men, contemners of virtue, beholding the good hap of another with an ill eye, favouring the more weak and the more wicked, and wishing all ill they can to men of honour they know not wherefore, except it be because they are honourable and well spoken of by others.

Treacherous and untrue, amplifying reports, smothering of truths, and always making things greater than they are, without faith, without hold. The faith or promise of a people, and the thought of a child, are of like durance, which change not only as occasions change, but according to the difference of those reports that every hour of the day may bring forth.

Mutinous, desiring nothing but novelties and changes, seditious, enemies to peace and quietness especially when they meet with a leader: for then even as the calm sea, of nature tumbleth, and foameth, and rageth, being stirred with the fury of the winds, so do the people swell, and grow proud, wild, and outragious. But take from them their leader, they become deject, grow wild, are confounded with astonishment.

Procurers and favourers of broils and alterations in household affairs, they account modesty simplicity, wisdom rusticity; and contrariwise, they give to fiery and heady violence the name of valour and fortitude. They prefer those that have hot heads and active hands before those that have a settled and temperate judgement, and upon whom the weight of the affairs must lie; boasters and pratlers before those that are simple and staid.

They care neither for the public good nor common honesty, but their private good only; and they refuse no base offices for their gain and commodity.

Always muttering and murmuring against the state, always belching out slanders and insolent speeches against those that govern and command. The meaner and poorer sort have no better pastime than to speak ill of the great and rich, not upon cause and reason, but of envy, being never content with their governors, nor the present state.

They have nothing but a mouth, they have tongues that cease not, spirits that budge not. They are a monster whose parts are all tongues, they speak all things, but know nothing; they look upon all, but see nothing; they laugh at all, and weep at all; fit to mutiny and rebel, not to fight. Their property is rather to assay to shake off their yoke, than to defend their liberty.

They never know how to hold a measure, nor to keep an honest mediocrity. Either like slaves they serve over-basely, or like lords they are beyond all measure insolent and tyrannical. They can not endure a soft and temperate bit, nor are pleased with a lawful liberty; they run always to extremities, either out of hope too much trusting, or too much distrusting out of fear. They will make you afeard, if you fear not them; when they are frighted, you chuck them under the chin, and you leap with both feet upon their bellies. They are audacious and proud, if a man show not the cudgel; and therefore the proverb is, 'tickle them, and they will prick thee; prick them, and they will tickle thee'. . . .

To conclude, the people are a savage beast; all that they think, is vanity; all they say, is false and erroneous; that they reprove, is good; that they approve, is naught; that which they praise is infamous; that which they do and undertake, is folly. The vulgar multitude is the mother of ignorance, injustice, inconstancy, idolatry, vanity, which never yet could be pleased: their motto is, *vox populi, vox Dei* [the voice of the people is the voice of God]; but we may say, *vox populi, vox stultorum* [the voice of the people is the voice of fools].

> Pierre Charron, *Of Wisdome* (1601, trans. 1606),
> pp.198-201.

Charron's prejudices are shared by the legal writer William Fulbecke. In appealing to history in support of his claim that democracy is 'no form of commonwealth' Fulbecke uses the same simile of the body and its members that Shakespeare uses in *Coriolanus*.

Democracy I have always taken contrary to the ancient division of monarchy, aristocracy, etc. to be no form of a commonwealth, if it be properly taken for the equal sway of the people without any superiority. For the heel can not stand in place of the head, unless the body be destroyed and the anatomy monstrous. It is against the nature of the people to bear rule, for they are as unfit for regiment as a mad man to give counsel, which Anarchis well perceiving did laugh at the assemblies and councils of the Athenians, because they did commit the sum of their affairs to the people's fury; and Xenophon writeth thus of the Athenian, that is, his own commonwealth: 'I can not allow the state of the Athenians because they embrace that form of commonwealth in which wicked and lewd persons do more flourish than good men and innocent'. . . .

They that are not virtuous, can not judge of them that be virtuous, and if they can not judge of them, how can they with conscience praise them: and if not them, how can they with safe conscience praise others? Is it not therefore a madness to gape for their suffrage, which are incompetent judges, and to care for their controlment which are unsensible censors . . .?

This beast of many heads hath a three-forked tongue: with the one part it tickleth the ears of them whom they flatter; with the other it licketh their wounds; with the last and sharpest it pricketh their hearts; with the first they flatter them, lulling their senses with fair words, and with soft speeches sliding into the bosom by forgeries and fables; with the other they lick their wounds, excusing their crimes, extenuating their faults, cooling and calming their rage that are incensed against them; with the third they prick: for let the popular idol be once crushed, none will sooner tread upon him than the people.

William Fulbecke, *The Pandectes of the Law of Nations* (1602), Sigs Hiv^v-Iii^v.

Fulbecke makes it clear why Elizabethans did not share our faith in democracy. Given the analogical model of the universe to which not only Coriolanus (III.i.154-5), but even the republican Brutus subscribes, it would have been illogical for them to have done so. If a man who allows his passions to rule his reason is, in Brutus' words, 'Like to a little kingdom' suffering 'The nature of an insurrection' (*Julius Caesar*, II.i.68-9), then it follows on his own analogy, that the irrational elements of society must similarly be controlled by what Menenius calls a 'kingly crowned head'. Thus even the radical Robert Parsons argues that 'of all other governments the monarchy is the best' (p.20).

But while monarchists like Merbury claimed absolute powers for the crown, in reality those powers were strictly limited. In the year following Elizabeth's coronation John Aylmer defined proleptically the terms of royal authority:

> The regiment of England is not a mere monarchy, as some for lack of consideration think, nor a mere oligarchy, nor democracy, but a rule mixed of all these, wherein each one of these have or should have like authority. The image whereof, and not the image, but the thing indeed, is to be seen in the parliament house, wherein you shall find these three estates: the king or queen, which representeth the monarchy; the noble men, which be the aristocracy; and the burgesses and knights the democracy. The very same had Lacedemonia, the noblest and best city governed that ever was. They had their kings, their senate and Hippagretes, which were for the people. As in Lacedemonia none of these could make or break laws, order for war or peace, or do anything without the other, the king nothing without the senate and commons, nor either of them or both without the king (albeit the senate and the Ephori had greater authority than the king had). In like manner, if the parliament use their privileges, the king can ordain nothing without them. If he do, it is his fault in usurping it, and their folly in permitting it. Wherefore in my judgement those that in King Henry the VIII's days, would not grant him that his proclamations should have the force of statute were good fathers of the country, and worthy commendation in defending their liberty. . . .
>
> It is not in England so dangerous a matter, to have a woman ruler, as men take it to be. For first, it is not she that ruleth but the laws, the executors whereof be her judges, appointed by her, her justices of peace and such other officers. But she may err in choosing such; so may a king. And therefore they have their counsel at their elbow, which by travel abroad, know men how fit or unfit they be for such offices. Second, she maketh no statutes or laws, but the honourable court

of Parliament; she breaketh none, but it must be she and they together or else not. Third, if she should judge in capital crimes, what danger were there in her womanish nature? None at all. For the verdict is the twelve men, which pass upon life and death, and not her's. Only this belongeth to her ministry, that when they have found treason, murder, or felony, she utter the pain limited in the law for that kind of trespass. Yea but this she can not do because a woman is not learned in the laws. No more is your king, and therefore have they their ministers, which can skill if they be cruel, wicked, handmakers, and bribers. It is their fault, and not the prince's unless he know them to be such and wink at it. What may she do alone wherein is peril? She may grant pardon to an offender: that is her prerogative, wherein if she err it is a tolerable and pitiful error to save life. She may misspend the revenues of the crown wantonly, so can kings do too, and commonly do, and yet may they be kings. If on the other part, the regiment were such, as all hanged upon the king's or queen's will, and not upon the laws written; if she might decree and make laws alone, without her senate; if she judged offences according to her wisdom, and not by limitation of statutes and laws; if she might dispose alone of war and peace; if to be short she were a mere monarch, and not a mixed ruler, you might peradventure make me to fear the matter the more, and the less to defend the cause. But the state being as it is or ought to be (if men were worth their ears) I can see no cause of fear, nor good reason why Saint Paul forbidding her to preach, should be thought to forbid her to rule.

John Aylmer, *An Harborowe for Faithfull and Trewe Subjectes* (1559), Sigs Hii^v-Hiv.

Ostensibly a defence of the principle of female sovereignty, Aylmer's pamphlet is actually a carefully worded warning to the young queen against the temptation of arrogating to herself autocratic powers. The English constitution, he says, is not a mere, or absolute, monarchy (Latin *merus*, pure), but a mixture of three kinds of government. The mixed constitution which incorporates elements of monarchy, aristocracy and democracy has a long history in political theory and was regarded by such classical writers as Aristotle (384-322 BC), Polybius (c.200-118 BC) and Cicero (106-43 BC) as the ideal form of government. Plutarch attributes the supposed unique stability of the mixed constitution to the fact that a middle element was held in balance between two extremes (Z.S. Fink, *The Classical Republicans*, p.9).

In Renaissance Europe it was widely believed that the supreme example in the modern world of a mixed state was Venice. Gaspar Contarini's treatise on the Venetian constitution explains that the equilibrium of the Venetian state is due to the fact that its government is based on the laws of nature.

> Every institution and government of man, the nearer it aspireth to the praise of perfection and goodness, the nearer should it imitate nature, the best mother of all things. For so hath she disposed the order of the whole world, that those things which are devoid of sense and understanding, should be ruled and governed by those that have sense and knowledge. And therefore in this assembly of men, which of us is called city, old men ought to be preferred before the younger sort, as those that are less subject to the perturbations of the mind, and withal having been of longer life, must needs be of greater experience in the affairs of the world. Therefore Aristotle in his *Politics* most wisely saith, that in every commonwealth which would emulate and follow the wisdom and policy of nature, old men should be placed at the helm, and the office of the young men should be to obey and to execute those things, which the old men should command them.
>
> With this reason therefore was the Senate ordained and established in this commonwealth of ours, and likewise the council of the ten, who in the city of Venice in whose commonwealth there is a mixture of the three governments royal, popular, and noble, do represent the state of the nobility, and are, as it were,

the mean or middle, which reconcileth and bindeth together the two extremes, that is, the popular estate represented in the great council, and the prince bearing a show of royalty. So saith Plato are the extreme elements, the earth and the fire, joined and bound together with the middle elements, as in a well tuned diapason the extreme voices are concorded together by the middle tunes of the diatessaron and diapente [as in a well tuned musical scale the octaves are harmonised by the intervals of the fourth and the fifth].

> Gaspar Contarini, *The Commonwealth and Government of Venice* (1543, trans. 1599), pp.64-5.

From plays like *The Merchant of Venice* and *Volpone* we derive a popular image of Venice as a devil's metropolis of rapacious materialism; beside this view we must set the equally popular idea of a city of 'palaces, towers and pinnacles reaching up into the clouds . . . as it were entertaining a league of intelligence with the heavenly powers' (contemporary translator's introduction to Contarini, Sig. Aiii). Of these two views it is the latter which is closer to the Venice of *Othello;* indeed Venice forms an essential part of the play's symbolic structure. While Othello struggles to control the darker side of his nature the same battle between civilisation and unreason is enacted on a larger scale in the war between Venice and the Turks (traditional symbol in Christian Europe of barbarism). As the Venetian senate considers the deceptive movements of the Turkish fleet, its cautious deliberations contrast ironically with Othello's disastrously impulsive action later in the play.

> *Duke.* There is no composition in these news
> That gives them credit.
> 1 *Sen.* Indeed, they are disproportion'd;
> My letters say a hundred and seven galleys.
> *Duke.* And mine a hundred and forty.
> 2 *Sen.*   And mine two hundred.
> But though they jump not on a just account—
> As in these cases, where the aim reports,
> 'Tis oft with difference—yet do they all confirm

A Turkish fleet, and bearing up to Cyprus.
Duke. Nay, it is possible enough to judgement.
I do not so secure me in the error
But the main article I do approve
In fearful sense.
Sailor. [*Within*] What, ho! what, ho! what, ho!

Enter Sailor.

Officer. A messenger from the galleys.
Duke.   Now, what's the business?
Sail. The Turkish preparation makes for Rhodes;
So was I bid report here to the state
By Signior Angelo.
Duke. How say you by this change?
1 Sen.   This cannot be,
     By no assay of reason. 'Tis a pageant
To keep us in false gaze. When we consider
The importancy of Cyprus to the Turk,
And let ourselves again but understand
That as it more concerns the Turk than Rhodes,
So may he with more facile question bear it,
For that it stands not in such warlike brace,
But altogether lacks th' abilities
That Rhodes is dress'd in–if we make thought of this,
We must not think the Turk is so unskilful
To leave that latest which concerns him first,
Neglecting an attempt of ease and gain
To wake and wage a danger profitless.
Duke. Nay, in all confidence, he's not for Rhodes.
Officer. Here is more news.

Enter a Messenger.

Mess. The Ottomites, reverend and gracious,
Steering with due course toward the isle of Rhodes,
Have there injointed them with an after fleet.
1 Sen. Ay, so I thought. How many, as you guess?
Mess. Of thirty sail; and now they do restem
Their backward course, bearing with frank
     appearance

> Their purposes toward Cyprus. Signior Montano,
> Your trusty and most valiant servitor,
> With his free duty recommends you thus,
> And prays you to believe him.
> *Duke.* 'Tis certain, then, for Cyprus.
>
> *Othello*, I.iii.1-43.

In representing the Venetian senate as a ruling council impartially and judiciously debating matters of state security Shakespeare reflects the moderate political views of writers like Sir Thomas Smith, who places great emphasis on the processes of consultation and debate in his account of the Elizabethan parliament. Although Smith declares that England is neither an aristocracy, nor a democracy, but a monarchy (p.56), he is in effect describing a mixed constitution.

> The most high and absolute power of the realm of England, is in the parliament. For as in war where the king himself in person, the nobility, the rest of the gentility, and the yeomanry is, there is the force and power of England, so in peace and consultation where the prince is to give life, and the last and highest commandment, the barony for the nobility and lords, the knights, esquires, gentlemen and commons for the lower part of the commonwealth, the bishops for the clergy be present to advertise, consult and show what is good and necessary for the commonwealth, and to consult together, and upon mature deliberation every bill or law being thrice read and disputed upon in either house, the other two parts first each a part and after the prince himself in presence of both the parties doth consent unto and alloweth. That is the prince's and whole realm's deed, whereupon justly no man can complain, but must accommodate himself to find it good and obey it.
>   That which is done by this consent is called firm, stable, and sanctum, and is taken for law. The parliament abrogateth old laws, maketh new, giveth orders for things past, and for things hereafter to be followed, changeth rights, and possessions of private

men, legitimateth bastards, establisheth forms of religion, altereth weights and measures, giveth forms of succession to the crown, defineth of doubtful rights, whereof is no law already made, appointeth subsidies, tails [levies], taxes, and impositions, giveth most free pardons and absolutions, restoreth in blood and name as the highest court, condemneth or absolveth them whom the prince will put to that trial. And to be short, all that ever the people of Rome might do either in *centuriatis, comitiis* or *tributis*, the same may be done by the parliament of England, which representeth and hath the power of the whole realm both the head and the body. For every Englishman is intended to be there present, either in person or by procuration and attornies, of what preeminence, state, dignity, or quality soever he be, from the prince (be he king or queen) to the lowest person of England. And the consent of the parliament is taken to be every man's consent.

Sir Thomas Smith, *De Republica Anglorum*
(1583), pp.78-9

As we shall see in Chapter 3, Shakespeare's successful rulers are notable for their willingness to consult with the commons. Conversely, where civil order breaks down altogether, especially in *Julius Caesar* and *Coriolanus*, it is significant that political leaders are shown as failing to consult openly and frankly. To see these plays as defences either of republicanism or of absolute monarchy is wrong. Shakespeare is not a political propagandist; he is interested in human beings caught up in the drama of power. However, it is important to bear in mind that the constitutional issues which form the background of that drama are not essentially 'simple' (E.M.W. Tillyard, *Shakespeare's History Plays*, p.64), but were the subject of vigorous contemporary debate.

3 The Just Ruler

Heated as the debate on royal prerogative became in the later years of Elizabeth's reign, few writers questioned the principle of monarchy itself. Given the organicist model of society to which even the most radical thinkers of the period generally subscribed, it was indeed the only logical form of government. Sir John Hayward sums up the familiar analogical argument for monarchy with exemplary simplicity when he writes: 'As one God ruleth the world, one master the family . . . so it seemeth no less natural that one state should be governed by one commander' (*An Answer to the First Part of a Conference Concerning Succession* (1603), Sig. Bi^v).

With almost universal agreement on the desirability of monarchical rule, whether absolute or constitutional, much of the political writing of the period concerned itself, not with alternative forms of government, but with the problem of defining the nature of the ideal prince. On this question there was a wealth of authoritative opinion available to the contemporary writer. Ancient and medieval political treatises often took the form of a *speculum principis,* or prince's mirror, in which the education, virtues and responsibilities of kings were analysed. The most influential of the Renaissance treatises on kingship was Erasmus's *The Education of a Christian Prince,* a work with which Shakespeare was almost certainly familiar. In his introductory chapter Erasmus warns the prince of his awesome responsibility.

> The instruction of the prince in accordance with established principles and ideas must take precedence over all else so that he may gain his knowledge from theory and not experience. Long experience which youth precludes will be supplied by the advice of older men.
>
> Do not think you may do anything you please, as foolish women and flatterers are in the habit of telling

princes. School yourself so that nothing pleases you which is not suitable. Remember that what is proper for private citizens, is not necessarily becoming in you. What is just a little mistake on the part of anyone else, is a disgrace in connection with a prince. The more others allow you, the less you should permit yourself. As others indulge you, so you should check yourself. Even when everyone marks you with approval, be your own severest critic. Your life is open to all – you cannot hide yourself. You have either to be a good man for the common good, or a bad one, bringing general destruction. As more honours are heaped upon you by everyone, you must make a special effort to see that you deserve them. No fitting honours or gratitude can ever be shown a good prince; no punishment can be bad enough for an evil prince. There is nothing in life better than a wise and good monarch; there is no greater scourge than a foolish or a wicked one. The corruption of an evil prince spreads more swiftly and widely than the scourge of any pestilence. In the same proportion a wholesome life on the part of the prince is, without question, the quickest and shortest way to improve public morals. The common people imitate nothing with more pleasure than what they see their prince do. Under a gambler, gambling is rife; under a warrior, everyone is embroiled; under an epicure, all disport in wasteful luxury; under a debauché, licence is rampant; under a cruel tyrant, everyone brings accusations and false witness. Go through your ancient history and you will find the life of the prince mirrored in the morals of his people. No comet, no dreadful power affects the progress of human affairs as the life of the prince grips and transforms the morals and character of his subjects.

Desiderius Erasmus, *The Education of a Christian Prince* (1516), pp.156-7.

The dependence of the state on the integrity of its prince is a central theme not only of Shakespeare's tragedies and histories, but also of plays like *Measure for Measure* and *The Tempest*. Rosencrantz's words in the third act of *Hamlet* reflect the conventional wisdom embodied in Erasmus's treatise.

> *Ros.* The single and peculiar life is bound
> With all the strength and armour of the mind
> To keep itself from noyance; but much more
> That spirit upon whose weal depends and rests
> The lives of many. The cease of majesty
> Dies not alone, but like a gulf doth draw
> What's near it with it. It is a massy wheel,
> Fix'd on the summit of the highest mount,
> To whose huge spokes ten thousand lesser things
> Are mortis'd and adjoin'd; which when it falls,
> Each small annexment, petty consequence,
> Attends the bois'trous ruin. Never alone
> Did the king sigh, but with a general groan.
>
> *Hamlet*, III.iii.11-23.

But there is another side to this argument. If the prince's subjects depend on him for their welfare, he must rely on them for advice and counsel. In the following passage from *The Boke Named The Governour* Sir Thomas Elyot, under the guise of offering general maxims about the nature of government, is in effect tactfully urging Henry VIII to heed the advice of his court.

> There be both reasons and examples, undoubtedly infinite, whereby may be proved that there can be no perfect public weal without one capital and sovereign governor which may long endure or continue. But since one mortal man can not have knowledge of all things done in a realm or large dominion, and at one time discuss all controversies, reform all transgressions, and exploit all consultations concluded as well for outward as inward affairs, it is expedient and also needful that under the capital governor be sundry mean [intermediary] authorities, as it were aiding him in the distribution of justice in sundry parts of a huge

multitude, whereby his labours being levigate and made more tolerable, he shall govern with the better advice, and consequently with a more perfect governance. And, as Jesus Sirach saith, the multitude of wise men is the wealth of the world. They which have such authorities to them committed may be called inferior governors, having respect to their office or duty, wherein is also a representation of governance, albeit they be named in Latin magistrates. And hereafter I intend to call them magistrates, lacking another more convenient word in English; but that will I do in the second part of this work, where I purpose to write of their sundry offices or effects of their authority. But for as much as in this part I intend to write of their education and virtue in manners, which they shall have in common with princes, in as much as thereby they shall, as well by example as by authority, order well them, which by their capital governor shall be to their rule committed, I may without annoyance of any man, name them governors at this time, appropriating to their sovereigns, names of kings and princes, since of a long custom these names in common form of speaking be in a higher preeminence and estimation than governors. That in every common weal ought to be a great number of such manner of persons it is partly proved in the chapter next before written, where I have spoken of the commodity of order. Also reason and common experience plainly declareth that, where the dominion is large and populous, there is it convenient that a prince have many inferior governors, which be named of Aristotle his eyes, ears, hands, and legs, which if they be of the best sort, as he furthermore saith, it seemeth impossible a country not to be well governed by good laws. And except excellent virtue and learning do inhabit a man of the base estate of the commonalty, to be thought of all men worthy to be so much advanced; else such governors would be chosen out of that estate of men which be called worshipful, if among them may be found a sufficient number, ornate with virtue and wisdom, meet for such purpose, and that for sundry causes.

Sir Thomas Elyot, *The Boke Named The Governour*,
pp. 15-17.

Elyot's point is made in a more forthright manner by his contemporary Thomas Starkey in his *Dialogue Between Pole and Lupset*. Passages such as the following make it clear why the *Dialogue* was never published in Starkey's own lifetime.

> Forasmuch as the great parliament should never be called but only at the election of our prince, or else for some other great urgent cause concerning the common state and policy, I would think it well if that at London should ever be remaining (because it is the chief city of our realm) the authority of the parliament, which ever there should be ready to remedy all such causes, and repress seditions, and defend the liberty of the whole body of the people at all such time as the king or his council tended to anything hurtful and prejudicial to the same. This council and authority of parliament should rest in these persons: first, in four of the greatest and ancient lords of the temporalty; two bishops, as of London and Canterbury; four of the chief judges; and four of the most wise citizens of London. These men jointly together should have authority of the whole parliament in such time as the parliament were dissolved.
>
> This authority should be chiefly instituted to this end and purpose: to see that the king and his proper council should do nothing against the ordinance of his laws and good policy; and they should have also power to call the great parliament whensoever to them it should seem necessary for the reformation of the whole state of the commonalty.

Thomas Starkey, *Dialogue Between Reginald Pole and Thomas Lupset*, p.155.

In the light of the emphasis which many writers of the period place on the importance of consultation between a ruler and his parliament, it is no doubt significant that the first action of Shakespeare's most successful king on ascending the throne is to summon parliament and 'choose such limbs of noble counsel/That the great body of our state may go/In equal rank with the best govern'd nation'. As Hal announces to the court his intended reformation of character he promises to accept his former enemy the Lord Chief Justice as his political mentor.

> There is my hand.
> You shall be as a father to my youth;
> My voice shall sound as you do prompt mine ear;
> And I will stop and humble my intents
> To your well-practis'd wise directions.
> And, Princes all, believe me, I beseech you,
> My father is gone wild into his grave,
> For in his tomb lie my affections;
> And with his spirits sadly I survive,
> To mock the expectation of the world,
> To frustrate prophecies, and to raze out
> Rotten opinion, who hath writ me down
> After my seeming. The tide of blood in me
> Hath proudly flow'd in vanity till now.
> Now doth it turn and ebb back to the sea,
> Where it shall mingle with the state of floods,
> And flow henceforth in formal majesty.
> Now call we our high court of parliament;
> And let us choose such limbs of noble counsel,
> That the great body of our state may go
> In equal rank with the best govern'd nation;
> That war, or peace, or both at once, may be
> As things acquainted and familiar to us;
> In which you, father, shall have foremost hand.
> Our coronation done, we will accite,
> As I before rememb'red, all our state;
> And–God consigning to my good intents–
> No prince nor peer shall have just cause to say,
> God shorten Harry's happy life one day.

2 Henry IV, V.ii.117-145.

The question of how to curb royal authority naturally tends to acquire importance in people's minds at times when the crown appears to be claiming new or excessive powers. Among the rights assumed by Henry VIII at the Reformation were those of secular head of the church. In the Act of Supremacy of 1534 he was accorded 'all honours, dignities, preeminences, jurisdictions, privileges, authorities, immunities, profits and commodities, to the . . . dignity of supreme head of the . . . Church belonging and appertaining' (G.R. Elton, *The Tudor Constitution* p.355). The prince's new role in the religious affairs of the nation and the struggle which this precipitated between church and crown may be seen anachronistically in the opening scene of *Henry V* with its hints of submerged political conflicts.

> *Cant.* My lord, I'll tell you: that self bill is urg'd
> Which in th' eleventh year of the last king's reign
> Was like, and had indeed against us pass'd
> But that the scambling and unquiet time
> Did push it out of farther question
> *Ely.* But how, my lord, shall we resist it now?
> *Cant.* It must be thought on. If it pass against us,
> We lose the better half of our possession;
> For all the temporal lands which men devout
> By testament have given to the church
> Would they strip from us; being valu'd thus–
> As much as would maintain, to the King's honour,
> Full fifteen earls and fifteen hundred knights,
> Six thousand and two hundred good esquires;
> And, to relief of lazars and weak age,
> Of indigent faint souls, past corporal toil,
> A hundred alms-houses right well supplied;
> And to the coffers of the King, beside,
> A thousand pounds by th' year: thus runs the bill.
> *Ely.* This would drink deep.
> *Cant.*   'Twould drink the cup and all.
> *Ely.* But what prevention?
> *Cant.* The King is full of grace and fair regard.
> *Ely.* And a true lover of the holy Church.
> *Cant.* The courses of his youth promis'd it not.
> The breath no sooner left his father's body
> But that his wildness, mortified in him,
> Seem'd to die too; yea, at that very moment,
> Consideration like an angel came
> And whipp'd th' offending Adam out of him,

Leaving his body as a paradise
T' envelop and contain celestial spirits.
Never was such a sudden scholar made;
Never came reformation in a flood,
With such a heady currance, scouring faults;
Nor never Hydra-headed wilfulness
So soon did lose his seat, and all at once,
As in this king.
Ely. We are blessed in the change.
Cant. Hear him but reason in divinity,
And all-admiring, with an inward wish
You would desire the King were made a prelate;
Hear him debate of commonwealth affairs,
You would say it hath been all in all his study;
List his discourse of war, and you shall hear
A fearful battle rend'red you in music.
Turn him to any cause of policy,
The Gordian knot of it he will unloose,
Familiar as his garter; that, when he speaks,
The air, a charter'd libertine, is still,
And the mute wonder lurketh in men's ears
To steal his sweet and honey'd sentences;
So that the art and practic part of life
Must be the mistress to this theoric;
Which is a wonder how his Grace should glean it,
Since his addiction was to courses vain,
His companies unletter'd, rude, and shallow,
His hours fill'd up with riots, banquets, sports;
And never noted in him any study,
Any retirement, any sequestration
From open haunts and popularity.

Henry V, I.i.1-59.

Any audience listening to such an encomium would naturally be curious to see whether reality matched the ideal. Looked at from one point of view, Shakespeare's King Henry seems the perfect textbook monarch; looked at from another, however, he appears at times almost like a parody of the Christian prince. In his honest concern for the welfare of his subjects Henry displays the traditional virtues of the responsible ruler. As he anticipates the Battle of Agincourt, he reflects on the cares of his office.

Upon the King! Let us our lives, our souls,
Our debts, our careful wives,
Our children, and our sins, lay on the King!
We must bear all. O hard condition,
Twin-born with greatness, subject to the breath
Of every fool, whose sense no more can feel
But his own wringing! What infinite heart's ease
Must kings neglect that private men enjoy!
And what have kings that privates have not too,
Save ceremony–save general ceremony?
And what art thou, thou idol Ceremony?
What kind of god art thou, that suffer'st more
Of mortal griefs than do thy worshippers?
What are thy rents? What are thy comings-in?
O Ceremony, show me but thy worth!
What is thy soul of adoration?
Art thou aught else but place, degree, and form,
Creating awe and fear in other men?
Wherein thou art less happy being fear'd
Than they in fearing.
What drink'st thou oft, instead of homage sweet,
But poison'd flattery? O, be sick, great greatness,
And bid thy ceremony give thee cure!
Thinks thou the fiery fever will go out
With titles blown from adulation?
Will it give place to flexure and low bending?
Canst thou, when thou command'st the beggar's knee,
Command the health of it? No, thou proud dream,
That play'st so subtly with a king's repose.
I am a king that find thee; and I know
'Tis not the balm, the sceptre, and the ball,
The sword, the mace, the crown imperial,
The intertissued robe of gold and pearl,
The farced title running fore the king,
The throne he sits on, nor the tide of pomp
That beats upon the high shore of this world–
No, not all these, thrice gorgeous ceremony,
Not all these, laid in bed majestical,
Can sleep so soundly as the wretched slave
Who, with a body fill'd and vacant mind,
Gets him to rest, cramm'd with distressful bread;

1. Encounter between European explorers and Florida Indians in 1564. Travellers' accounts of the New World stimulated debate on primitivism and the values of the civilised world.

3. Woodcut from John Foxe's *Book of Martyrs* (1554). While successive government pamphlets emphasised the terrible penalties of rebellion, radical writers continued to assert the rights of subjects to resist unjust authority.

'Tis I alone can teach you to make warre,
I know what greatest Conquerirs knew, & are.
I fill the Breasts of greatest Potentates.
I give them lawes to governe their Estates.

2. Niccolo Machiavelli (1469-1527). His most famous work, *The Prince*, overturned traditional ideas about the character and virtues necessary in a good ruler.

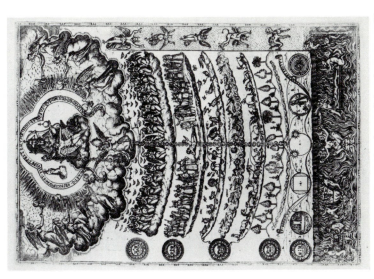

4. Title page of Raleigh's providentialist *The History of the World* (1614). A new generation of historians was beginning to concern itself less with the religious than with the political lessons to be learned from a study of the past.

5. The Great Chain of Being. As the traditional cosmos with its orderly system of interlocking hierarchies began to be demolished, sceptical writers questioned the notion of a universal law of nature implanted by God in man's heart.

6. The 1985 Royal Shakespeare Company production of *Richard III* at the Barbican with Antony Sher as the dying Richard.

Never sees horrid night, the child of hell;
But, like a lackey, from the rise to set
Sweats in the eye of Phoebus, and all night
Sleeps in Elysium; next day, after dawn,
Doth rise and help Hyperion to his horse;
And follows so the ever-running year
With profitable labour, to his grave.
And but for ceremony, such a wretch,
Winding up days with toil and nights with sleep,
Had the fore-hand and vantage of a king.
The slave, a member of the country's peace,
Enjoys it; but in gross brain little wots
What watch the king keeps to maintain the peace
Whose hours the peasant best advantages.

Henry V, IV.i.226-80.

For all its troubled sincerity Henry's soliloquy is substantially traditional in the way it portrays the cares of princely office. The great Flemish humanist Justus Lipsius, for example, in his *Sixe Bookes of Politickes* rehearses the commonplace that the prince must watch while his subjects sleep.

In this one thing especially, a king differeth from a tyrant, that a tyrant regardeth only, and seeketh after his own commodity, and a king the profit and good of his subjects, who is the right pastor of the people, as Homer termeth him. Wherefore whosoever thou art that art graced with this high title, consider that the thraldom of thy subjects is not committed unto thee, but their liberty, defence, and protection. Neither is the commonwealth thine, but thou art the commonwealth's.

Hear what a poet saith: thou oughtest to take upon thee the charge and office of a good citizen and father; to provide for all, not for thyself; and not to be moved so much for thine own private, as for the public loss. He is an evil governor, who of a large and ample fortune, can not gather any other profit than the usurpation of licentiousness; who taketh no care how matters pass, but playeth the prince in voluptuousness and lust. But a just and good king laboureth, watcheth, and knoweth that the greatest empire is accompanied with greatest cares. His vigilance preserveth his subjects when they are asleep; his labour giveth them their ease; his industry and travail, maintaineth their pleasures; his care in his charge, their rest and quiet. Wherefore, he may sometimes pause and refresh himself, but never be dissolute and careless.

This he ought to do for his own good, and for the benefit of his subjects, for the greatness of the prince is then well grounded and established when all his subjects shall perceive he is not only over them, but for them.

Justus Lipsius, *Six Bookes of Politickes or Civil Doctrine* (1589, trans. 1594), p.23.

Lipsius later explains how before battle the prince must exhort and encourage his men.

Always thou oughtest to labour that thy army be in a readiness before thine enemies, for two respects: . . . First, because thou mayest the rather accomplish, what thou deemest best to be done, when there is no man to let [hinder] thee. Next, that thereby thou encreasest the confidence and courage of thine own soldiers, and dost lessen the virtue and value of the enemy, because they seem always to be the strongest, who provoke others with a resolution. Commonly he that assaileth hath more value in him than he that is put to defend himself.

Likewise it helpeth very much if both before the battle, and in the fight, the general do cheerfully show the value of his mind both in countenance and with his eyes. For what dare they enterprise if they see thee slothful, and as it were out of thy wits, running with open cries here and there? Truly, of necessity they must make themselves ready to run away when they see their captain in desperation. Thou oughtest to stir up their courage, and to instruct them, to the end that,

where there is least cause of fear, there may be least
assurance of danger. Who so contemneth death, it
flieth from him; and he that feareth it, it followeth
him. In battles they are always in most danger who
dread most; resolution is as a wall or rampart. The
slothful frame not the destinies unto themselves as
they list, but esteeming long life to be the chiefest
felicity, they are often oppressed with death.

Justus Lipsius, *Sixe Bookes of Politickes or Civil
Doctrine,* p.173.

In this respect too, Henry can hardly be faulted. His
stirring speech at the siege of Harfleur is a model of martial
rhetoric.

Once more unto the breach, dear friends, once more;
Or close the wall up with our English dead.
In peace there's nothing so becomes a man
As modest stillness and humility;
But when the blast of war blows in our ears,
Then imitate the action of the tiger:
Stiffen the sinews, summon up the blood,
Disguise fair nature with hard-favour'd rage;
Then lend the eye a terrible aspect;
Let it pry through the portage of the head
Like the brass cannon; let the brow o'erwhelm it
As fearfully as doth a galled rock
O'erhang and jutty his confounded base,
Swill'd with the wild and wasteful ocean.
Now set the teeth and stretch the nostril wide;
Hold hard the breath, and bend up every spirit
To his full height. On, on, you noblest English,
Whose blood is fet from fathers of war-proof—
Fathers that like so many Alexanders
Have in these parts from morn till even fought,
And sheath'd their swords for lack of argument.
Dishonour not your mothers; now attest
That those whom you call'd fathers did beget you.
Be copy now to men of grosser blood,
And teach them how to war. And you, good yeomen,
Whose limbs were made in England, show us here

> The mettle of your pasture; let us swear
> That you are worth your breeding–which I doubt
>   not;
> For there is none of you so mean and base
> That hath not noble lustre in your eyes.
> I see you stand like greyhounds in the slips,
> Straining upon the start. The game's afoot:
> Follow your spirit; and upon this charge
> Cry 'God for Harry, England, and Saint George!'
>
> *Henry V*, III.i.1-34.

But while some critics have seen *Henry V* as a model dramatisation of Renaissance treatises on war, others have questioned the motives for Henry's campaign against the French, seeing it not as a just war, but as an act of policy designed to win him honour and renown, and, by busying 'giddy minds/With foreign quarrels' (*2 Henry IV*, IV.v.214-5), to strengthen a dubious title to the throne. It has been pointed out (A. Gurr, '*Henry V* and the Bees' Commonwealth', pp.61-3) that, while Shakespeare was almost certainly familiar with *The Education of a Christian Prince*, and echoes many of its precepts in his portrayal of Henry V, Erasmus himself could never have condoned the war against France. In the final chapter of his book Erasmus argues that attempts to extend territory are always self-defeating.

> Nothing is dearer to a good prince than to have the best possible subjects. But what greater or more ready ruin to moral character is there than war? There is nothing more to the wish of the prince than to see his people safe and prospering in every way. But while he is learning to campaign he is compelled to expose his young men to so many dangers, and often in a single hour to make many and many an orphan, widow, childless old man, beggar, and unhappy wretch.
> The wisdom of princes will be too costly for the world if they persist in learning from experience how dreadful war is, so that when they are old men, they may say: 'I did not believe that war was so utterly destructive!' But – and I call God to witness – with

what countless afflictions on the whole world have you learned that idea! The prince will understand some day that it was useless to extend the territory of the kingdom and that what in the beginning seemed a gain was [in reality] tremendous loss, but in the meantime a great many thousands of men have been killed or impoverished. These things should better be learned from books, from the stories of old men, from the tribulations of neighbours: 'For many years this or that prince has been fighting on for such and such a kingdom. How much more is his loss than his gain!' Let the good prince establish matters of the sort that will be of lasting worth. Those things which are begun out of a fancy are to our liking while the fancy lasts, but the things which are based on judgement and which delight the young man, will also afford pleasure to the old man. Nowhere is this truth more to be observed than in the beginning of war. . . .

The Christian prince should first question his own right, and then if it is established without a doubt he should carefully consider whether it should be maintained by means of catastrophes to the whole world. Those who are wise sometimes prefer to lose a thing rather than to gain it, because they realise that it will be less costly. Caesar, I think, would prefer to give up his rights rather than seek to attain the old monarchy and that right which the letter of the jurisconsults conferred on him. But what will be safe, they say, if no one maintains his rights? Let the prince insist by all means, if there is any advantage to the state, only do not let the right of the prince bear too hard on his subjects. But what is safe anywhere while everyone is maintaining his rights to the last ditch? We see wars arise from wars, wars following wars, and no end or limit to the upheaval! It is certainly obvious that nothing is accomplished by these means. Therefore other remedies should be given a trial. Not even between the best of friends will relations remain permanently harmonious unless sometimes one gives in to the other. A husband often makes some concession to his wife so as not to break their harmony. What does war cause but war? Courtesy, on the other hand, calls forth courtesy, and fairness, fairness. The fact that he can see from the countless calamities which war always carries in its wake, that the greatest hardship falls on those to whom the war means nothing and who are in no way deserving of these catastrophes, will have an effect on the devoted and merciful prince.

After the prince has reckoned and added up the total of all the catastrophes [which would come] to the world (if that could ever be done), then he should think over in his own mind: 'Shall I, one person, be the cause of so many calamities? Shall I alone be charged with such an outpouring of human blood; with causing so many widows; with filling so many homes with lamentation and mourning; with robbing so many old men of their sons; with impoverishing so many who do not deserve such a fate; and with such utter destruction of morals, laws, and practical religion? Must I account for all these things before Christ?' The prince cannot punish his enemy unless he first brings hostile activities upon his own subjects. He must fleece his people, and he must receive [into his realm] the soldier, who has been called ruthless (and not without justification) by Virgil. He must cut off his subjects from those districts which they formerly enjoyed for their own advantage; [or else the reverse], he must shut up his subjects in order to hem in the enemy. And it frequently happens that we inflict worse sufferings upon our own people than upon the enemy. It is more difficult, as well as more desirable, to build a fine city than to destroy it. But we see flourishing cities which are established by inexperienced and common people, demolished by the wrath of princes. Very often we destroy a town with greater labour and expense than that with which we could build a new one, and we carry on war at such great expense, such loss, such zeal, and pains, that peace could be maintained at one-tenth of these costs.

Let the good prince always lean toward that glory which is not steeped in blood nor linked with the misfortune of another. In war, however fortunately it turns out, the good fortune of one is always the ruin of the other. Many a time, too, the victor weeps over a victory bought too dearly.

Desiderius Erasmus, *The Education of a Christian Prince*, pp.250-4.

In the light of Erasmus's Christian pacifism Henry's warning to the citizens at Harfleur of soldiers 'rough and hard of heart' 'mowing like grass/Your fresh-fair virgins and your flowering infants' (III.iii.11-14) strikes a sharply discordant note. Must we then assume that Shakespeare is writing with sustained and bitter irony in his portrayal of Henry as 'no tyrant, but a Christian king' (I.ii.241)? The answer is probably no: the overall tone of the play does not support such a view. What is clear, however, from a study of the historical context in which plays like *Henry V* were written is the complexity of Shakespeare's response to political questions. Above all he is a relentless critic of sentimental self-deception. *Henry V* contains some wonderfully stirring rhetoric; but the play does not allow us to forget the cruel and sometimes futile realities of war.

Since classical antiquity political writers had defined the ideal ruler by comparing him with his opposite, the tyrant. The object of the *speculum principis* was not only to instruct through praise, but also to caution through negative example. The following passage from a political treatise by the influential 16th-century French thinker, Jean Bodin, offers a classic contrast between the just ruler and the tyrant.

Lest the good should be confused and so confounded with the bad; or that we should under the name of a tyrant comprehend them also which were right worthy and famous men, let us compare the worst tyrant with the best king, that by such comparison of the two extremes, those may be the better perceived which are in the middest betwixt both. Now when I say the best king, my meaning is after the common manner; neither do I seek after such a one as is accomplished with all heroical virtues; or the rare paragon of justice, wisdom, and religion, a man without all imputation, which in the fables of ancient worthies, were propounded with more magnificence than truth, for princes to look upon and to imitate, such as never was, nor ever shall be; but rather such an example of a good and just king, as is indeed in the rank of princes to be found; and such a one as is always ready to bestow his goods, his blood, and life, for the good of his people.

Now the greatest difference betwixt a king and a tyrant is, for that a king conformeth himself unto the laws of nature, which the tyrant at his pleasure treadeth under foot: the one of them respecteth religion, justice, and faith; whereas the other regardeth neither God, faith, nor law. The one of them referreth all his actions to the good of the commonwealth, and safety of his subjects; whereas the other respecteth nothing more than his own particular profit, revenge, or pleasure. The one doth all his endeavour for the enriching of his subjects; whereas the other seeketh after nothing more than by the impoverishment of them, to encrease his own wealth. The one of them accounteth his own goods to be the goods of his people; the other reckoneth not only the goods, but even the bodies of his subjects also to be his own. The one of them severely revengeth the public injuries done against the state, and easily pardoneth the wrongs done unto himself; the other most cruelly revengeth his own, and pardoneth that which is done against others. The one easily forgiveth the offences of other men, but is of his own misdeeds a severe judge; whereas the other most sharply revenges even the least offences of others, but is unto himself most favourable. The one of them favoureth the honour of modest matrons, and other men's wives; the other triumpheth in their shame and dishonour. The one refuseth not to be freely and discreetly reproved for that he hath done amiss; the other hateth nothing more than the grave free-spoken man. The one enforceth himself to maintain and keep his subjects in peace and unity: whereas the other seeketh still to set them at odds, so to ruinate them one by another, and with the confiscation of their lands and goods to enrich himself. The one taketh pleasure to see his subjects, and to be of them oftentimes seen and heard; whereas the other feareth their presence, and hideth himself from them, as from his enemies. The one reposeth his estate and fealty [feudal loyalty] in their love towards him; the other in their fear. The one taketh no care but for his subjects; the other feareth nothing more than them. The one chargeth his subjects as little as he can, neither exacteth any thing of them, but when the public necessity so requireth; whereas the other drinketh his subjects blood, gnaweth their bones, and out of them also sucketh even the marrow, so by all means seeking to weaken them. The one advanceth unto the highest degrees of honour the best and most virtuous men; whereas the other still promoteth the greatest thieves and villains, whom he may use as sponges, to suck up the wealth of his subjects. The one frankly bestoweth the greatest and most gainful offices of the state upon men of best deserts, who, free from bribery and corruption, may defend the people from all injury and oppression; whereas the other setteth the same to sale to such as will give most for them, so by their robberies and unreasonable exactions, to keep the people under, and then afterward when they are well fatted, to cut such caterpillars throats also, so to be accounted great justicers. The one measureth his manners according unto his laws; the other measureth his laws according to his own disposition and pleasure. The one is ready to expose his life for the good of his country and people; the other wisheth it and them all to perish for himself. The one is beloved and honoured of his subjects; the other hateth them all, and is likewise of them hated. The one in time of war hath no recourse but unto his own subjects; whereas the other hath no greater wars than against them. The one hath neither guard, nor garrison, but of his own people; whereas the other for the defence of his person, and keeping of his subjects in awe, hath always a garrison of armed strangers to go before him. The one liveth secure in all quiet and tranquillity of mind; the other troubled with careful and contrary thoughts, still anguishing in perpetual fear. The one expecteth a most blessed and eternal life in heaven; the other still fearing everlasting pains of hell. The one hath the immortal good author of all his actions; the other followeth the advice of wicked men and damned spirits. In brief the one is praised and honoured of all men whilst he liveth, and much missed after his death; whereas the other is defamed yet living, and most shamefully reviled both by word and writing when he is dead. And albeit that a tyrant abound in wealth, have honour, sovereignty, health, and surpassing champion-like strength of body, with the deep and profound knowledge of many and great matters, and flowing eloquence most of tyrants to be in others feared; yet shall he therefore be never the better, but well the worse; abusing his wealth to fulfil his lust; his sovereignty, to the oppressing of other men's liberty; his strength for the performing of his villainy; and his knowledge for the circumventing of the plain and simple, and shameful confusion of all things. Which so many and notable gifts, if they chance by the grace and goodness of God to be given to any good prince, we then esteem of him, as of a God, sent even down from heaven into the earth here and amongst us.

Jean Bodin, *The Sixe Bookes of a Commonweale*
(1576, trans. 1606), pp.211-13.

Measured against these criteria the conduct of Shakespeare's Richard II can only be described as tyrannous.

North. Now, afore God, 'tis shame such wrongs are borne
   In him, a royal prince, and many moe
   Of noble blood in this declining land.

The King is not himself, but basely led
By flatterers; and what they will inform,
Merely in hate, 'gainst any of us all,
That will the King severely prosecute
'Gainst us, our lives, our children, and our heirs.
Ross. The commons hath he pill'd with grievous
   taxes;
And quite lost their hearts; the nobles hath he fin'd
For ancient quarrels and quite lost their hearts.
Willo. And daily new exactions are devis'd,
As blanks, benevolences, and I wot not what;
But what, a God's name, doth become of this?
North. Wars hath not wasted it, for warr'd he hath
   not,
But basely yielded upon compromise
That which his noble ancestors achiev'd with blows.
More hath he spent in peace than they in wars.
Ross. The Earl of Wiltshire hath the realm in farm.
Willo. The King's grown bankrupt like a broken man.
North. Reproach and dissolution hangeth over him.
Ross. He hath not money for these Irish wars,
His burdenous taxations notwithstanding,
But by the robbing of the banish'd Duke.

Richard II, II.i.238-61.

In the 16th century popular thinking on the subject of tyranny was coloured by an image of corruption based, not so much on the works, as on the reputation of the great Italian political thinker Machiavelli. In a pamphlet entitled *A Discourse upon the Meanes of Wel Governing . . . Against Nicholas Machiavell* a French writer compares the courts of France and England in the latter part of the century.

When our countrymen's minds were sick, and corrupted with these pestilent diseases, and that discipline waxed stale, then came forth the books of Machiavelli, a most pernicious writer, which began not in secret and stealing manner but by open means, and as it were a continual assault, utterly destroyed, not this or that virtue, but even all virtues at once, insomuch as it took faith from the princes; authority and majesty from laws; liberty from the people; and peace and concord from all persons, which are the only remedies for present maladies. For what shall I speak of religion, whereof the Machiavellans had none, as already plainly appeareth; yet they greatly laboured also, to deprive us of the same . . .?

Truly it is a wonderful thing to consider how fast that evil weed hath grown within these four years, seeing there is almost none that striveth to excel in virtue or knowledge; as though the only way to obtain honour and riches were by this deceiver's direction. But now to turn mine eyes from beholding so many miseries of poor afflicted France, as often as I see or remember our neighbour countries (which thing I do daily) so often do I bewail our miseries. Yet am I right joyful for your felicity, chiefly because God of His great bounty, hath given you a most renowned queen, as well in deed, as title, even in the midst of so many troubles. For she [Elizabeth I] coming to the crown, even when England was tossed with tempestuous storms, so dispersed those clouds, with the brightness of her counsel and countenance, that no civil dissention, nor external invasion hath disturbed your peace and tranquillity these many years, especially so many wars sounding on every side. For she, by maintaining wholesome unity amongst all degrees, hath hitherto preserved the state of her realm, not only safe but flourishing; not by Machiavellian arts as guile, perfidy, and other villanies practising, but by true virtues as clemency, justice, faith. Therefore goeth she her progress through her realm of England, entertained in all places with happy applause, rejoicing, and prosperity of all her subjects, she being a princess, of both nobles and commons, by due desert most entirely beloved. Whereas we against our wills behold our country swimming in blood, and disfigured by subversion, which is a joyful object to the eyes of strangers, yea and those [who] labour most to work her destruction, who should be most careful to rescue and deliver poor France out of her long calamities. But the Lord will at length behold our miseries. But O how happy are ye, both because you have so gracious a queen, and also for that the infectious Machiavellian doctrine, hath not breathed nor penetrated the entrails of most happy England.

> Innocent Gentillet, *A Discourse upon the Meanes of Wel Governing . . . Against Nicholas Machiavell* (1576, trans. 1602), Sigs ¶iii^v-¶iv.

This is the popular image of Machiavelli. However, more profound thinkers than Gentillet were well aware of Machiavelli's revolutionary importance as a political theorist. His most famous, though by no means his most important, work, *The Prince,* bears little similarity to a book like Erasmus's *The Education of a Christian Prince.* Machiavelli is above all a pragmatist. Appealing not to an abstract theological principle, but to the practical realities of political life, he set out in *The Prince* to offer advice on the art of successful government. Politics, says Machiavelli, is a deceitful business. It is not enough to rely on the traditional kingly virtues of justice and integrity; to be successful the prince must learn to beat the world at its own game.

> How commendable in a prince it is to keep his word, and live with integrity, not making use of cunning and subtlety, every one knows well. Yet we see by experience in these our days, that those princes have effected great matters, who have made small reckoning of keeping their words, and have known by their craft to turn and wind men about, and in the end, have overcome those who have grounded upon the truth. You must then know, there are two kinds of combating or fighting: the one by right of the laws, the other merely by force. That first way is proper to men, the other is also common to beasts; but because the first many times suffices not, there is a necessity to make recourse to the second; wherefore it behoves a prince to know how to make good use of that part which belongs to a beast, as well as that which is proper to a man. This part hath been covertly shown to princes by ancient writers, who say that Achilles and many others of those ancient princes were

intrusted to Chiron the senator, to be brought up under his discipline: the moral of this, having for their teacher one that was half a beast and half a man, was nothing else, but that it was needful for a prince to understand how to make his advantage of the one and the other nature, because neither could subsist without the other. A prince, then, being necessitated to know how to make use of that part belonging to a beast, ought to serve himself of the conditions of the fox and the lion; for the lion cannot keep himself from snares, nor the fox defend himself against the wolves. He had need then be a fox, that he may beware of the snares, and a lion that he may scare the wolves. Those that stand wholly upon the lion, understand not well themselves. And therefore a wise prince cannot, nor ought not keep his faith given, when the observance thereof turns to disadvantage, and the occasions that made him promise are past. For if men were all good, this rule would not be allowable; but being they are full of mischief, and would not make it good to thee, neither art thou tied to keep it with them. Nor shall a prince ever want lawful occasions to give colour to this breach. Very many modern examples hereof might be alleged, wherein might be shown how many peaces concluded, and how many promises made, have been violated and broken by the infidelity of princes; and ordinarily things have best succeeded with him that hath been nearest the fox in condition. But it is necessary to understand how to set a good colour upon this disposition, and to be able to feign and dissemble thoroughly; and men are so simple, and yield so much to the present necessities, that he who hath a mind to deceive, shall always find another that will be deceived. . . . Therefore is there no necessity for a prince to be endued with all above written qualities, but it behoveth well that he seem to be so; or rather I will boldly say this, that having these qualities, and always regulating himself by them, they are hurtful; but seeming to have them, they are advantageous; as to seem pitiful, faithful, mild, religious, and of integrity, and indeed to be so;

provided withal thou beest of such a composition,
that if need require to use the contrary, thou canst,
and knowest how to apply thy self thereto. And it
suffices to conceive this, that a prince, and especially a
new prince, cannot observe all those things, for which
men are held good; he being often forced, for the
maintenance of his state, to do contrary to his faith,
charity, humanity, and religion. And therefore it
behoves him to have a mind so disposed, as to turn
and take the advantage of all winds and fortunes; and
as formerly I said, not forsake the good, while he can;
but to know how to make use of the evil upon
necessity.

Machiavelli, *The Prince* (1514, trans. 1640), pp.321-3.

A measure of the respect with which Machiavelli's ideas
were received by serious thinkers is the fact that by the latter
part of the 16th century even the more conservative writers
may be found echoing his words. The pious and scholarly
Lipsius is an example.

It be sometimes lawful, and reasonable to trace out
indirect courses in this tempestuous sea of the affairs
of the world; and if we can not arrive at the haven by
the right course, that we turn sail, and alter our
navigation to attain thereunto. Who will blame me so
far herein, or demand the cause why I forsake virtue?
Wine, although it be somewhat tempered with water,
continueth to be wine: so doth prudence not change
her name, albeit a few drops of deceit be mingled
therewith. For I always mean but a small deal, and to
a good end: mothers and physicians, do they not
often deceive little children, to the end they might
beguile their improvident age by a deceitful taste, and
the deceit may not be perceived? And why should not
a prince do the like towards the simple people, or
towards some other prince his neighbour? Surely
when one is not strong enough to debate the matter, it
is not amiss secretly to entrap. And as the King of
Sparta teacheth us, where we cannot prevail by the

lion's skin, we must put on the fox's. I will always with Pindar praise him, who in matters of variance doth make show to have the courage of a lion, but in consultation is as crafty as a fox. Be thou the like in time and place, and careless of that these young men do say at school, or within doors, whom I know not to be capable hearers of civil doctrine, and much less judges. And surely this tribunal seat requireth a man who is not ignorant of those things which happen in this life. Of such a person we shall easily obtain this; neither will he so strictly condemn the Italian fault-writer, (who poor soul is laid at of all hands) and as a holy person saith, that there is a certain honest and laudable deceit.

> Justus Lipsius, *Six Bookes of Politickes or Civil Doctrine*, p.114.

Of all Shakespeare's characters none illustrates better the principle of 'laudable deceit' than Prince Hal. Behind the carefully cultivated image of the mad-cap prince indulging in wild and irresponsible pranks there is an astute and calculating mind. In the first act of *I Henry IV*, Hal reveals in soliloquy his essentially Machiavellian temperament.

> I know you all, and will awhile uphold
> The unyok'd humour of your idleness;
> Yet herein will I imitate the sun,
> Who doth permit the base contagious clouds
> To smother up his beauty from the world,
> That, when he please again to be himself,
> Being wanted, he may be more wond'red at
> By breaking through the foul and ugly mists
> Of vapours that did seem to strangle him.
> If all the year were playing holidays,
> To sport would be as tedious as to work;
> But when they seldom come, they wish'd for come,
> And nothing pleaseth but rare accidents.
> So, when this loose behaviour I throw off
> And pay the debt I never promised,
> By how much better than my word I am,
> By so much shall I falsify men's hopes;

And, like bright metal on a sullen ground,
My reformation, glitt'ring o'er my fault,
Shall show more goodly and attract more eyes
Than that which hath no foil to set it off.
I'll so offend to make offence a skill,
Redeeming time when men think least I will.

I Henry IV, I.ii.188-210.

The ruthlessness with which Hal rejects Falstaff at the end of Part II is entirely in keeping with the unsentimental view of politics revealed in his opening soliloquy. Like the use of calculated deception, the willingness to use ruthless measures to secure political advantage in a just cause is something which even the most conservative writers of the period advocate. Bodin writes in his *The Six Bookes of a Commonweale*:

Things oft times fall out, that for the variety of times, places, persons, and other occasions presenting themselves, princes are constrained to do such things, as may seem unto them tyrannical, and unto others commendable. Wherefore let no man measure tyranny by severity, which is often times in a prince most necessary. ... Neither are those murders, proscriptions, banishments, incests, ravishments, and other such villanies which happen in civil wars, in the changing or destruction of the states of common-weals, or the establishment of the same, to be called tyrannies: for that in such violent conversion and change of state, it cannot otherwise be.
    Now to the contrary it happeneth often that the state of a city or commonweal ruinated by the too much lenity and facility of one prince, is again relieved and upholden by the austere severity of another. It is sufficiently known how terrible the tyranny of Domitian was unto the senate, the nobility, and other great lords and governors of the Roman Empire, insomuch that all his laws and edicts were by their procurement after his death repealed. And yet for all that he was even after his death also

most highly by the general consent of all the provinces commended. For that the proconsuls with the other magistrates and officers of the commonweal were never before more upright or freer from corruption than they were in his time, for fear they had of his security. . . . Also when a prince with most sharp severity as with a bridle keepeth in the minds and licentious desires of a furious and headstrong people, as if it were an untamed beast: such wholesome severity ought in no wise to be accounted or called tyranny; but to the contrary Cicero calleth such licentious liberty of the unruly people mere [complete] tyranny.

Now they that praise the goodness, bounty, and courtesy of a prince, without wisdom are themselves unwise and ignorant in matters of state, abusing therein both their praises and leisure, forasmuch as such simplicity without wisdom is most dangerous and pernicious unto a king, and much more to be feared than is the great severity of a cruel, covetous, and inaccessible prince. So that it seemeth our ancient fathers not without cause to have used this proverb, that of a crafty and subtle man is made a good king, which saying unto the delicate ears of such as measure all things by false opinions rather than by sound reasons, may seem right strange. For by the too much sufferance and simplicity of too good a king, it cometh to pass that flatterers, extortioners, and men of most wicked disposition, without respect, enjoy the principal honours, offices, charges, benefits, and preferments of the commonwealth, spoiling the revenues of the state, whereby the poor people are gnawn unto the very bones, and cruelly made slaves unto the great, insomuch as that instead of one tyrant, there is ten thousand. Out of which corruption also of the magistrates, and too much courtesy of the king proceed many mischiefs and evils, as impunity of offenders, or murderers, and oppressors, for that the king so good and so gracious cannot refuse to grant them pardon. In brief, under such a prince the public good is turned into particular, and all the charge falleth upon the poor people.

Jean Bodin, *The Six Bookes of a Commonweale*,
pp.216-7.

Similar arguments in defence of the ruthless suppression of insurrection are presented dramatically in the symbolic garden scene in the third act of *Richard II*. The conversation which Queen Isabel and her ladies overhear as they walk in the royal garden is fully of heavy innuendo.

> *Queen.* But stay, here come the gardeners.
> Let's step into the shadow of these trees.
> My wretchedness unto a row of pins,
> They will talk of state, for every one doth so
> Against a change; woe is forerun with woe.
> [*Queen and ladies retire.*]
> *Gard.* Go, bind thou up yon dangling apricocks,
> Which, like unruly children, make their sire
> Stoop with oppression of their prodigal weight;
> Give some supportance to the bending twigs.
> Go thou, and like an executioner
> Cut off the heads of too fast growing sprays
> That look too lofty in our commonwealth;
> All must be even in our government.
> You thus employ'd, I will go root away
> The noisome weeds which without profit suck
> The soil's fertility from wholesome flowers.
> *Serv.* Why should we, in the compass of a pale,
> Keep law and form and due proportion,
> Showing, as in a model, our firm estate,
> When our sea-walled garden, the whole land,
> Is full of weeds; her fairest flowers chok'd up,
> Her fruit trees all unprun'd, her hedges ruin'd,
> Her knots disordered, and her wholesome herbs
> Swarming with caterpillars?
> *Gard.*   Hold thy peace.
>   He that hath suffer'd this disorder'd spring
> Hath now himself met with the fall of leaf;
> The weeds which his broad-spreading leaves did
>   shelter,

That seem'd in eating him to hold him up
Are pluck'd up root and all by Bolingbroke–
I mean the Earl of Wiltshire, Bushy, Green.
Serv. What, are they dead?
Gard.   They are; and Bolingbroke
    Hath seiz'd the wasteful king. O, what pity is it
That he had not so trimm'd and dress'd his land
As we this garden! We at time of year
Do wound the bark, the skin of our fruit trees,
Lest, being over-proud in sap and blood,
With too much riches it confound itself;
Had he done so to great and growing men,
They might have liv'd to bear, and he to taste
Their fruits of duty. Superfluous branches
We lop away, that bearing boughs may live;
Had he done so, himself had borne the crown,
Which waste of idle hours hath quite thrown down.

Richard II, III.iv.24-66.

But Richard is not simply a weak and ineffectual king like
Henry VI: he is a tyrant – at least according to most
contemporary definitions of the term – who thinks more
about his own needs than his country's. Whether it is right to
depose such a king and replace him by Act of Parliament with
a more just and capable ruler, or whether, as Richard himself
believes, his subjects owe him absolute obedience as God's
vicegerent was a political question which aroused fiercer
controversy amongst Elizabethans than any other.

4 Rebellion

A central concern of Shakespeare's two English historical tetralogies is the question of the rights of subjects to judge and if necessary depose their rulers. For a generation which had not only witnessed a growing power struggle between Elizabeth and her parliaments, but was, in the words of a contemporary foreign observer, 'shaken by religious feuds, by plagues and other internal troubles' (*Calendar of State Papers* (Venice) 1592-1603, p.119), the deposition of Richard II in 1399 and the dynastic quarrels this led to were of immediate topical interest. As the Queen herself remarked when a play (probably Shakespeare's) dealing with these events was revived shortly before the Essex rebellion in 1601, 'I am Richard II: know ye not that?' (quoted by J.E. Neale, *Queen Elizabeth*, p.381).

In Elizabethan England debate on the rights of subjects to challenge royal authority takes the traditional form of discussion of the remedies for tyranny. Medieval writers, while strongly deprecating rebellion, had usually conceded that a king who violated his coronation oath could no longer expect obedience from his subjects. St Thomas Aquinas argues that, while it may be more expedient for subjects to tolerate a mild form of tyranny than to rebel, deposition of tyrannical rulers is justifiable in extreme cases.

> If to provide itself with a king belongs to the right of a given multitude, it is not unjust that the king be deposed or have his power restricted by that same multitude if, becoming a tyrant, he abuses the royal power. It must not be thought that such a multitude is acting unfaithfully in deposing the tyrant, even though it had previously subjected itself to him in perpetuity, because he himself has deserved that the covenant with his subjects should not be kept, since, in ruling the multitude, he did not act faithfully as the

office of a king demands. Thus did the Romans, who had accepted Tarquin the Proud as their king, cast him out from the kingship on account of his tyranny and the tyranny of his sons; and they set up in their place a lesser power, namely, the consular power. Similarly Domitian, who had succeeded those most moderate emperors, Vespasian, his father, and Titus, his brother, was slain by the Roman senate when he exercised tyranny, and all his wicked deeds were justly and profitably declared null and void by a decree of the senate. Thus it came about that Blessed John the Evangelist, the beloved disciple of God, who had been exiled to the island of Patmos by that very Domitian, was sent back to Ephesus by a decree of the senate.

St Thomas Aquinas, *On Kingship: To the King of Cyprus* (1266), p.27.

Aquinas is here concerned with the blatant abuse of royal power. However with the Reformation and the rise of a number of strong religious minorities tyranny acquired a new meaning: the term tended now to be applied by any dissenting body to a prince who refused it the right to practise what it believed was the true religion. To protect itself from the threat of counter-reform the Tudor establishment promulgated a doctrine of non-resistance. When, following the suppression of the Northern Rebellion of 1569, a papal bull was issued (1570) excommunicating Elizabeth and claiming to absolve her subjects from allegiance, the Queen and her Council issued a new homily 'Agaynst Disobedience and Wylful Rebellion'. (The original collection of homilies was published by Edward VI's regents in 1547.) This new homily asked the question, should subjects rebel against 'indiscreet and evil governors'? Its answer was unequivocal: rebellion was a crime against God which could never under any circumstances be justified.

What shall subjects do then? Shall they obey valiant, stout, wise, and good princes, and contemn, disobey, and rebel against children being their princes, or against indiscreet and evil governors? God forbid. For first what a perilous thing were it to commit unto the subjects the judgement which prince is wise and godly, and his government good, and which is otherwise, as though the foot must judge of the head, an enterprise very heinous, and must needs breed rebellion. For who else be they that are most inclined to rebellion, but such haughty spirits, from whom springeth such foul ruin of realms? Is not rebellion the greatest of all mischiefs? And who are most ready to the greatest mischiefs, but the worst men? Rebels therefore the worst of all subjects are most ready to rebellion, as being the worst of all vices, and furthest from the duty of a good subject, as on the contrary part, the best subjects are most firm and constant in obedience, as in the special and peculiar virtue of good subjects. What an unworthy matter were it then to make the naughtiest subjects, and most inclined to rebellion and all evil, judges over their princes, over their government and over their counsellors, to determine which of them be good or tolerable, and which be evil, and so intolerable that they must needs be removed by rebels, being ever ready as the naughtiest subjects, soonest to rebel against the best princes, specially if they be young in age, women in fear, or gentle and courteous in government, as trusting by their wicked boldness easily to overthrow their weaknesses and gentleness or at the least so to fear the minds of such princes that they may have impunity of their mischievous doings. But whereas indeed a rebel is worse than the worst prince, and rebellion worse than the worst government of the worst prince that hitherto hath been: both are rebels unmeet ministers, and rebellion an unfit and unwholesome medicine to reform any small lacks in a prince, or to cure any little griefs in government, such lewd remedies being far worse than any other maladies and disorders that can be in the body of a commonwealth. . . .

So remaineth it now that I partly do declare unto you what an abominable sin against God and man rebellion is, and how dreadfully the wrath of God is kindled and inflamed against all rebels, and what horrible plagues, punishments, and deaths, and finally eternal damnation doth hang over their heads; as how on the contrary part good and obedient subjects are in God's favour, and be partakers of peace, quietness, and security, with other God's manifold blessings in this world, and by His mercies through our saviour Christ, of life everlasting also in the world to come. How horrible a sin against God and man rebellion is, can not possibly be expressed according unto the greatness thereof. For he that nameth rebellion, nameth not a singular, or one only sin, as is theft, robbery, murder, and such like: but he nameth the whole puddle and sink of all sins against God and man, against his prince, his country, his countrymen, his parents, his children, his kinfolks, his friends, and against all men universally, all sins I say against God and all men heaped together nameth he, that nameth rebellion.

An Homilie Agaynst Disobedience and Wylful
Rebellion (1570), Sigs Bi-Bi^v; Div^v-Ei.

It is the same doctrine of non-resistance which Shakespeare puts into the mouth of John of Gaunt in the second scene of *Richard II*.

> *Gaunt.* Alas, the part I had in Woodstock's blood
> Doth more solicit me than your exclaims
> To stir against the butchers of his life!
> But since correction lieth in those hands
> Which made the fault that we cannot correct.
> Put we our quarrel to the will of heaven;
> Who, when they see the hours ripe on earth,
> Will rain hot vengeance on offenders' heads.
> *Duch.* Finds brotherhood in thee no sharper spur?
> Hath love in thy old blood no living fire?
> Edward's seven sons, whereof thyself art one,
> Were as seven vials of his sacred blood,
> Or seven fair branches springing from one root,

Some of those seven are dried by nature's course,
Some of those branches by the Destinies cut;
But Thomas, my dear lord, my life, my Gloucester,
One vial full of Edward's sacred blood,
One flourishing branch of his most royal root,
Is crack'd, and all the precious liquor split;
Is hack'd down, and his summer leaves all faded,
By envy's hand and murder's bloody axe.
Ah, Gaunt, his blood was thine! That bed, that
    womb,
That mettle, that self mould, that fashion'd thee,
Made him a man; and though thou livest and
    breathest,
Yet art thou slain in him. Thou dost consent
In some large measure to thy father's death
In that thou seest thy wretched brother die,
Who was the model of thy father's life.
Call it not patience, Gaunt–it is depair;
In suff'ring thus thy brother to be slaught'red,
Thou showest the naked pathway to thy life,
Teaching stern murder how to butcher thee.
That which in mean men we entitle patience
Is pale cold cowardice in noble breasts.
What shall I say? To safeguard thine own life
The best way is to venge my Gloucester's death.
Gaunt. God's is the quarrel; for God's substitute,
His deputy anointed in His sight,
Hath caus'd his death; the which if wrongfully,
Let heaven revenge; for I may never lift
An angry arm against His minister.

               Richard II, I.ii.1-41.

What Gaunt is expressing here is an essentially Tudor theory of absolute obedience. Although many 16th-century writers made similar claims, it was not until the end of the century that it began to be argued that kings had absolute authority over their subjects. Five years before his accession to the English throne James VI of Scotland (James I of England) published a book entitled *The Trew Law of Free Monarchies* in which he argued that kings were answerable only to God.

As there is not a thing so necessary to be known by the people of any land, next the knowledge of their God, as the right knowledge of their allegiance, according to the form of government established among them, especially in a monarchy (which form of government, as resembling the Divinity, approacheth nearest to perfection, as all the learned and wise men from the beginning have agreed upon, unity being the perfection of all things), so hath the ignorance, and (which is worse) the seduced opinion of the multitude blinded by them, who think themselves able to teach and instruct the ignorants, procured the wrack and overthrow of sundry flourishing commonwealths, and heaped heavy calamities, threatening utter destruction upon others. And the smiling success that unlawful rebellions have oftentimes had against princes in ages past (such hath been the misery, and iniquity of the time) hath by way of practice strengthened many in their error: albeit there cannot be a more deceivable argument than to judge ay the justness of the cause by the event thereof as hereafter shall be proved more at length. . . .

First then, I will set down the true grounds, whereupon I am to build, out of the scriptures, since monarchy is the true pattern of Divinity, as I have already said; next, from the fundamental laws of our own kingdom, which nearest must concern us. Kings are called gods by the prophetical King David, because they sit upon God His throne in the earth, and have the account of their administration to give unto Him. Their office is to minister justice and judgement to the people, as the same David saith; to advance the good, and punish the evil, as he likewise saith; to establish good laws to his people, and procure obedience to the same. . . . The kings in Scotland were before any estates or ranks of men within the same, before any parliaments were holden, or laws made. And by them was the land distributed (which at the first was wholly theirs), states erected and discerned, and forms of government devised and established. And so it follows of necessity, that the kings were the authors and makers of the laws, and not the laws of the kings.

According to these fundamental laws, we daily see that in the parliament (which is nothing else but the head court of the king and his vassals) the laws are but craved by his subjects, and only made by him at their rogation, and with their advice. For albeit the king made daily statutes and ordinances, enjoining such pains thereto as he thinks meet, without any advice of parliament or estates; yet it lies in the power of no parliament, to make any kind of law or statute, without his scepter be to it, for giving it the force of a law: . . .

Since I have so clearly proved then out of the fundamental laws and practice of this country, what right and power a king hath over his land and subjects, it is easy to be understood what allegiance and obedience his lieges owe unto him; I mean always of such free monarchies as our king is, and not of elective kings, and much less of such sort of governors as the dukes of Venice are, whose aristocratic and limited government is nothing like to free monarchies, although the malice of some writers hath not been ashamed to misknow any difference to be betwixt them. And if it be now lawful to any particular lords, tenants or vassals, upon whatsoever pretext, to control and displace their master, and overlord (as is clearer nor the sun by all laws of the world) how much less may the subjects and vassals of the great overlord the king control or displace him? And since in all inferior judgements in the land the people may not upon any respects displace their magistrates, although but subaltern. For the people of a borough cannot displace their provost before the time of their election; nor in ecclesiastical policy the flock can upon any pretence displace the pastor, nor judge of him. Yea even the poor schoolmaster cannot be displaced by his scholars. If these, I say (whereof some are but inferior, subaltern, and temporal magistrates, and none of them equal in any sort to the dignity of a king) cannot be displaced for any occasion or pretext by them that are ruled by them, how much less is it lawful upon any pretext to control or displace the great provost, and great schoolmaster of the whole land, except by inverting the order of all law and reason, the commanded may be made to command their commander, the judged to judge their judge, and they that are governed, to govern their time about their lord and governor.

James VI, *The Trew Law of Free Monarchies* (1598), pp.53-64.

Such exaggerated claims for the quasi-divine authority of the crown did not, of course, go unchallenged. It would be quite wrong, however, to suppose that those writers who reasserted the right to resist were atheists mounting a radical critique of the age's religious ideology. Serious arguments in support of the right to resist were in the 16th century always religious in essence: they constituted a plea for freedom of worship. One of the most vocal critics of the Elizabethan establishment was Robert Parsons. Without challenging the familiar analogical argument for monarchy, Parsons claims that 'princes have oftentimes by their commonwealths been lawfully deposed for misgovernment, and that God hath allowed and assisted the same'.

Not only hath the commonwealth authority to put back the next inheritors upon lawful considerations, but also to dispossess them that have been lawfully put in possession if they fulfil not the laws and conditions, by which and for which, their dignity was given them. Which point as it cannot serve for wicked men to be troublesome unto their governors for their own interests or appetites, so yet when it is done upon just and urgent causes and by public authority of the whole body, the justice thereof is plain, not only by the grounds and reasons before alleged, but also by those examples of the Romans and Grecians already mentioned, who lawfully deposed their kings upon such considerations, and changed also their monarchy and kingly government into other forms of regiment. And it might be proved also, by examples of all other nations, and this perhaps with a circumstance which I know not, whether every man here have considered the same, to wit, that God hath wonderfully concurred for the most part, with such judicial acts of the commonwealth against their evil princes, not only in prospering the same, but by giving them also commonly some notable successor in place of the deposed, thereby both to justify the fact, and to remedy the fault of him that went before . . . .

By this then you see the ground whereon dependeth the righteous and lawful deposition and chastisement of wicked princes, to wit their failing in their oath and promises, which they made at their first entrance, that they would rule and govern justly, according to law, conscience, equity, and religion, wherein when they fail, or wilfully decline, casting behind them all respect of obligation and duty to the end for which they were made princes and advanced in dignity above the rest, then is the commonwealth not only free from all oaths made by her of obedience or allegiance to such unworthy princes, but is bound moreover for saving the whole body, to resist, chasten and remove such evil heads, if she be able, for that otherwise all would come to destruction, ruin, and public desolation.

Robert Parsons, *A Conference About the Next Succession to the Crown of England*, pp. 32-3; 77-8.

Shakespeare's own interest in the question of rebellion may be seen not only in the two English tetralogies, but also in plays like *Julius Caesar* and *Hamlet*. Each play deals with the problem from a different point of view and each raises different issues. But perhaps the least ambiguous treatment of the subject is Richmond's oration to his troops in the final act of *Richard III*. Where the *Homilie Agaynst Disobedience and Wylful Rebellion* made it clear that tyrants were to be seen as God's way of punishing a wicked people and therefore never to be resisted, Henry, Early of Richmond claims, like Parsons, that tyrannicide may receive divine approval.

More than I have said, loving countrymen,

The leisure and enforcement of the time
Forbids to dwell upon; yet remember this:
God and our good cause fight upon our side;
The prayers of holy saints and wronged souls,
Like high-rear'd bulwarks, stand before our faces;
Richard except, those whom we fight against
Had rather have us win than him they follow.
For what is he they follow? Truly, gentlemen,
A bloody tyrant and a homicide;
One rais'd in blood, and one in blood establish'd;
One that made means to come by what he hath,
And slaughtered those that were the means to help
      him;
A base foul stone, made precious by the foil
Of England's chair, where he is falsely set;
One that hath ever been God's enemy.
Then if you fight against God's enemy,
God will in justice ward you as his soldiers;
If you do sweat to put a tyrant down,
You sleep in peace, the tyrant being slain;
If you do fight against your country's foes,
Your country's fat shall pay your pains the hire;
If you do fight in safeguard of your wives,
Your wives shall welcome home the conquerors;
If you do free your children from the sword,
Your children's children quits it in your age.
Then, in the name of God and all these rights,
Advance your standards, draw your willing swords.
For me, the ransom of my bold attempt
Shall be this cold corpse on the earth's cold face;
But if I thrive, the gain of my attempt
The least of you shall share his part thereof.
Sound drums and trumpets boldly and cheerfully;
God and Saint George! Richmond and victory!

Richard III, V.iii.237-70.

Where Shakespeare's own views lie is in this case clear. The newly crowned Henry VII is portrayed in his final speech as an instrument of destiny bringing peace to the divided houses of Lancaster and York through his marriage to Elizabeth.

But if *Richard III* clearly endorses the principle of

responsible tyrannicide, *Hamlet* suggests, though less unambiguously, that attempts to curb tyranny by personal means cannot be condoned. The ethical complexities of this question may be seen in Bishop Ponet's equivocations on the subject of private vengeance.

> Albeit some do hold that the manner and means to punish evil and evil doers is not all one among Christians, which be in deed that they profess in word, and ethnics [pagans], which think it lawful for every private man, without respect of order and time, to punish evil. Yet the laws of many Christian regions do permit that private men may kill malefactors, yea though they were magistrates in some cases: as when a governor shall suddenly run upon an innocent, or go about to shoot him through with a gun, or if he should be found in bed with a man's wife, or go about to deflower and ravish a man's daughter; much more if he go about to betray and make away his country to foreigners, etc. Nevertheless, forasmuch as all things in every Christian commonwealth ought to be done decently and according to order and charity, I think it cannot be maintained by God's word that any private man may kill, except (where execution of just punishment upon tyrants, idolators and traitorous governors is either by the whole state utterly neglected, or the prince with the nobility and council conspire the subversion or alteration of their country and people) any private man have some special inward commandment or surely proved motion of God (as Moses had to kill the Egyptians) or be otherwise commanded or permitted by common authority upon just occasion and common necessity to kill.

> John Ponet, *A Short Treatise of Politic Power* (1556), Sigs Gviii-Gviii^v.

Hamlet certainly has what Ponet calls 'some special inward commandment'; but it is by no means clear that this is a 'surely proved motion of God'. For although he proves to his own satisfaction that his father's ghost is telling him the truth, this is in itself no guarantee of its integrity. As Banquo says in

Macbeth: 'The instruments of darkness tell us truths,/Win us with honest trifles, to betray's/In deepest consequence' (I.iii.124-6). The most damning comment on the ghost and its incitement to private revenge is a scene which apparently has little to do with Hamlet himself. As we watch Claudius in Act IV, Scene vii appealing to Laertes's emotions and tempting him to avenge *his* father's murder by a further act of lawless violence we are inevitably reminded of the ghost's similar tactics in Act I, Scene v.

> *Laer.* And so have I a noble father lost;
> A sister driven into desp'rate terms,
> Whose worth, if praises may go back again,
> Stood challenger on mount of all the age
> For her perfections. But my revenge will come.
> *King.* Break not your sleeps for that. You must not
>   think
> That we are made of stuff so flat and dull
> That we can let our beard be shook with danger,
> And think it pastime. You shortly shall hear more.
> I lov'd your father, and we love our self;
> And that, I hope, will teach you to imagine–

*   *   *

> *King.* Laertes, was your father dear to you?
> Or are you like the painting of a sorrow,
> A face without a heart?
> *Laer.*   Why ask you this?
> *King.* Not that I think you did not love your father;
>   father;
> But that I know love is begun by time,
> And that I seem in passages of proof,
> Time qualifies the spark and fire of it.
> There lives within the very flame of love
> A kind of wick or snuff that will abate it;
> And nothing is at a like goodness still;
> For goodness, growing to a pleurisy,
> Dies in his own too much. That we would do,
> We should do when we would; for this 'would'
>   changes,

And hath abatements and delays as many
As there are tongues, are hands, are accidents;
And then this 'should' is like a spendthrift's sigh
That hurts by easing. But to the quick of th' ulcer:
Hamlet comes back; what would you undertake
To show yourself in deed your father's son
More than in words?
Laer.   To cut his throat i' th' church.
King. No place, indeed, should murder sanctuarize;
    sanctuarize;
Revenge should have no bounds. But, good Laertes,
Will you do this?

                    Hamlet, IV.vii.25-35; 107-129.

Both *Richard III* and *Hamlet* portray men who are unambiguous tyrants. While *Richard III* suggests that the prospect of a 'harvest of perpetual peace' justifies the risk of 'one bloody trial of sharp war' (V.ii.15-16), *Hamlet* implies that private acts of vengeance are likely to lead only to further 'carnal, bloody, and unnatural acts' (V.ii.373). With *Julius Caesar* the matter is complicated by the question of whether Caesar is to be seen as a tyrant who poses a serious threat to the freedom of the Roman people, or whether on the contrary he represents a principle of stability safeguarding the state against anarchy. In the 16th century both views were commonly expressed. Conscious of the parallels between Caesar and their own ageing, autocratic queen, Elizabethan writers naturally interpreted the history of the final years of republican Rome in the light of their own political sympathies.

The opening scenes of *Julius Caesar* lay stress on Caesar's physical and moral shortcomings: he is epileptic, he is deaf, he is proud and he is susceptible to flattery. Yet none of these things necessarily disqualifies him from exercising quasi-regal authority. Indeed contemporary writers make it clear that the individual is not to be confused with his office. Edmund Plowden, a lawyer, wrote in 1578:

The king has in him two bodies, viz. a body natural, and a body politic. His body natural (if it be considered in itself) is a body mortal, subject to all infirmities that come by nature or accident, to the imbecility of infancy or old age, and to the like defects that happen to the natural bodies of other people. But his body politic is a body that cannot be seen or handled, consisting of policy and government, and constituted for the direction of the people, and the management of the public weal, and this body is utterly void of infancy, and old age, and other natural defects and imbecilities which the body natural is subject to, and for this cause, what the king does in his body politic cannot be invalidated or frustrated by any disability in his natural body.

> Edmund Plowden, 'Report of a Case in the Court of the Duchy of Lancaster', *The Commentaries and Reports of Edmund Plowden* (1578), vol. II, fols 212a-213.

In the light of Plowden's distinction between the king's two 'bodies' – the one mystical and immutable, the other fallible and mortal – Caesar's repeated claims (in the scene leading up to his assassination) to immunity from normal passions begin to sound less arrogant.

> *Dec.* Where is Metellus Cimber? Let him go
> And presently prefer his suit to Caesar.
> *Bru.* He is address'd; press near and second him.
> *Cin.* Casca, you are the first that rears your hand.
> *Caes.* Are we all ready? What is now amiss
> That Caesar and his Senate must redress?
> *Met.* Most high, most mighty, and most puissant
>   Caesar,
> Metellus Cimber throws before thy seat
> An humble heart. [*Kneeling.*]
> *Caes.* I must prevent thee, Cimber.
> These couchings and these lowly courtesies
> Might fire the blood of ordinary men,
> And turn pre-ordinance and first decree
> Into the law of children. Be not fond
> To think that Caesar bears such rebel blood
> That will be thaw'd from the true quality
> With that which melteth fools–I mean, sweet words,

Low-crooked curtsies, and base spaniel fawning.
Thy brother by decree is banished;
If thou dost bend, and pray, and fawn for him.
I spurn thee like a cur out of my way.
Know, Caesar doth not wrong; nor without cause
Will he be satisfied.
Met. Is there no voice more worthy than my own
To sound more sweetly in great Caesar's ear
For the repealing of my banish'd brother?
Bru. I kiss thy hand, but not in flattery, Caesar,
Desiring thee that Publius Cimber may
Have an immediate freedom of repeal.
Caes. What, Brutus!
Cas.   Pardon, Caesar! Caesar, pardon!
   As low as to thy foot doth Cassius fall,
To beg enfranchisement for Publius Cimber.
Caes. I could be well mov'd, if I were as you;
If I could pray to move, prayers would move me;
But I am constant as the northern star,
Of whose true-fix'd and resting quality
There is no fellow in the firmament.
The skies are painted with unnumb'red sparks,
They are all fire, and every one doth shine;
But there's but one in all doth hold his place.
So in the world: 'tis furnish'd well with men,
And men are flesh and blood, and apprehensive;
Yet in the number I do know but one
That unassailable holds on his rank,
Unshak'd of motion; and that I am he,
Let me a little show it, even in this—
That I was constant Cimber should be banish'd,
And constant do remain to keep him so.
Cin. O Caesar!
Caes.   Hence! Wilt thou lift up Olympus?
Dec. Great Caesar!
Caes.   Doth not Brutus bootless kneel?
Casca. Speak, hands, for me!
[*They stab Caesar. Casca strikes the first, Brutus the
   last blow.*]
Caes. Et tu, Brute?—Then fall, Caesar! [*Dies.*]
Cin. Liberty! Freedom! Tyranny is dead!

Run hence, proclaim, cry it about the streets.
Cas. Some to the common pulpits, and cry out
'Liberty, freedom, and enfranchisement!'

Julius Caesar, III.i.27-81.

Whether or not Caesar is consciously appealing in his final speech to the traditional distinction between the king's two 'bodies', the result is the same: in assassinating Caesar the conspirators have destroyed not just a man, but an institution. In view of the civil chaos which ensues, their action would appear to confirm the traditional belief that 'to proceed against the cruelty of tyrants is an action to be undertaken, not through the private presumption of a few, but rather by public authority' (St Thomas Aquinas, *On Kingship*, p.27).

The play which presents the problem of rebellion in its most complex form is *Richard II*. From the frequency with which Elizabethan political pamphleteers refer to the events of 1399 it is clear that for them Richard's disposition was a kind of test case confirming or refuting the rights of subjects to judge their rulers. Modern interpretations of Shakespeare's play have been extensively influenced by a supposedly universally held Elizabethan belief in the sinfulness of disobedience. 'In doctrine the play is entirely orthodox,' writes Tillyard *(Shakespeare's History Plays*, p.261), 'Shakespeare knows that Richard's crimes never amounted to tyranny, and hence that outright rebellion against him was a crime.' This 'orthodox' view of Richard's deposition originates, Tillyard argues, in the 16th-century chronicles which Shakespeare used as his sources. However, when we read these histories we find, not a doctrinaire condemnation of Bolingbroke the usurper, but a careful record of the constitutional procedures involved in the voluntary transfer of power from Richard to Henry. The following is an abridgement of Raphael Holinshed's account of this process (Holinshed's *Chronicles* are Shakespeare's major source for *Richard II*).

The next day after his coming to London, the king from Westminster was had to the Tower, and there committed to safe custody. Many evil disposed persons, assembling themselves together in great numbers, intended to have met with him, and to have taken him from such as had the conveying of him, that they might have slain him. But the mayor and aldermen gathered to them the worshipful common-ers and grave citizens, by whose policy, and not without much ado, the other were revoked from their evil purpose; albeit, before they might be pacified, they coming to Westminster, took master John Sclake, dean of the king's chapel, and from thence brought him to Newgate, and there laid him fast in irons.

After this was a parliament called by the Duke of Lancaster, using the name of King Richard in the writs directed forth to the lords, and other states for their summons. This parliament began the thirteenth day of September, in the which many heinous points of misgovernance and injurious dealings in the administration of his kingly office were laid to the charge of this noble prince King Richard, the which (to the end the commons might be persuaded that he was an unprofitable prince to the commonwealth, and worthy to be deposed) were engrossed up in 33 solemn articles, heinous to the ears of all men, and to some almost incredible, the very effect of which articles here ensure, according to the copy which I have seen, as follows. [The articles of complaint against Richard are then listed, together with the Bill of Deposition. This is followed by Richard's own formal declaration of abdication.]

Now forthwith he subscribed the same, and after delivered it unto the Archbishop of Canterbury, saying that if it were in his power, or at his assignment, he would that the Duke of Lancaster there present should be his successor and king after him. And in token hereof, he took a ring of gold from his finger being his signet, and put it upon the said duke's finger, desiring and requiring the Archbishop of York, and the Bishop of Hereford, to show and make report unto the lords of the parliament of his voluntary resignation, and also of his intent and good mind that he bare towards his cousin the Duke of Lancaster, to have him his successor and their king after him. All this done every man took their leave and returned to their own.

Upon the morrow after being Tuesday, and the last day of September, all the lords spiritual and temporal, with the commons of the said parliament, assembled at Westminster, where, in the presence of them, the Archbishop of York, and the Bishop of Hereford, according to the king's request, showed unto them the voluntary renouncing of the king, with the favour also which he bare to his cousin of Lancaster to have him his successor. And moreover showed them the schedule or bill of renouncement, signed with King Richard's own hand, which they caused to be read first in Latin, as it was written, and after in English. This done, the question was first asked of the lords, if they would admit and allow the renouncement: the which when it was of them granted and confirmed, the like question was asked of the commons, and of them in like manner confirmed. [The declaration of Richard's deposition is then read out to parliament.]

Immediately as the sentence was in this wise passed, and that by reason thereof the realm stood void without head or governor for the time, the Duke of Lancaster rising from the place where before he sat, and standing where all those in the house might behold him in reverend manner made a sign of the cross on his forehead, and likewise on his breast, and after silence by an officer commanded, said unto the people there being present, these words following: 'The Duke of Lancaster layeth challenge or claim to the crown. In the name of the Father, and of the Son, and of the Holy Ghost, I, Henry of Lancaster, claim the realm of England and the crown, with all the appurtenances, as I that am descended by right line of the blood coming from that good lord King Henry III, and through the right that God of his grace hath sent me, with the help of my kin, and of my friends to recover the same, which was in point to be undone for default of good governance and due justice.'

After these words thus by him uttered, he returned

and sat him down in the place where before he had sat. Then the lords having heard and well perceived this claim thus made by this noble man, each of them asked of other what they thought therein. At length, after a little pausing or stay made, the Archbishop of Canterbury having notice of the minds of the lords, stood up and asked the commons if they would assent to the lords, which in their minds thought the claim of the duke made, to be rightful and necessary for the wealth of the realm and them all: whereto the commons with one voice cried, 'Yea, yea, yea.'

Raphael Holinshed, *Chronicles of England, Scotland, and Ireland* (1577), vol. II, pp.859-65.

For a playwright with a keen sense of the paradoxes of political life, it would have been difficult to find historical material with greater dramatic potential than this. Faced, not with conspiracy hiding 'in smiles and affability' (*Julius Caesar*, II.i.82), but with the united voice of the bishops, the lords and the commons, the rights of sovereignty are here put to the ultimate test. The intractable nature of the problem is caught in Shakespeare's vivid portrayal of Richard's emotional and intellectual confusion. At the same time that he acknowledges his guilt, freely nominating Bolingbroke as his worthy successor, he still clings desperately to his sentimental belief in the sanctity of kings.

> *K. Rich.* Give me the crown. Here, cousin, seize the crown.
> Here cousin,
> On this side my hand, and on that side thine.
> Now is this golden crown like a deep well
> That owes two buckets, filling one another;
> The emptier ever dancing in the air,
> The other down, unseen, and full of water.
> That bucket down and full of tears am I,
> Drinking my griefs, whilst you mount up on high.
> *Boling.* I thought you had been willing to resign.
> *K. Rich.* My crown I am; but still my griefs are mine.
> You may my glories and my state depose,
> But not my griefs; still am I king of those.

> *Boling.* Part of your cares you give me with your
> crown.
> *K. Rich.* Your cares set up do not pluck my cares
> down.
> My care is loss of care, by old care done;
> Your care is gain of care, by new care won.
> The cares I give I have, though given away;
> They tend the crown, yet still with me they stay.
> *Boling.* Are you contented to resign the crown?
> *K. Rich.* Ay, no; no, ay; for I must nothing be;
> Therefore no no, for I resign to thee.
> Now mark me how I will undo myself:
> I give this heavy weight from off my head,
> And this unwieldy sceptre from my hand,
> The pride of kingly sway from out my heart;
> With mine own tears I wash away my balm,
> With mine own hands I give away my crown,
> With mine own tongue deny my sacred state,
> With mine own breath release all duteous oaths;
> All pomp and majesty I do forswear;
> My manors, rents, revenues, I forgo;
> My acts, decrees, and statutes, I deny.
> God pardon all oaths that are broke to me!
> God keep all vows unbroke are made to thee!
> Make me, that nothing have, with nothing griev'd,
> And thou with all pleas'd, that hast all achiev'd.
> Long mayst thou live in Richard's seat to sit,
> And soon lie Richard in an earthy pit.
> God save King Henry, unking'd Richard says,
> And send him many years of sunshine days!
> What more remains?
> *North.*   No more; but that you read
> These accusations, and these grievous crimes
> Committed by your person and your followers
> Against the state and profit of his land;
> That, by confessing them, the souls of men
> May deem that you are worthily depos'd.
> *K. Rich.* Must I do so? And must I ravel out
> My weav'd-up follies? Gentle Northumberland,
> If thy offences were upon record,
> Would it not shame thee in so fair a troop

To read a lecture of them? If thou wouldst,
There shouldst thou find one heinous article,
Containing the deposing of a king
And cracking the strong warrant of an oath,
Mark'd with a blot, damn'd in the book of heaven.
Nay, all of you that stand and look upon me
Whilst that my wretchedness doth bait myself,
Though some of you, with Pilate, wash your hands,
Showing an outward pity—yet you Pilates
Have here deliver'd me to my sour cross,
And water cannot wash away your sin.

Richard II, IV.i.181-242.

Richard's conviction that a monarch can never be legitimately deposed is based on the theory that a king is 'the figure of God's majesty,/His captain, steward, deputy elect' (*Richard II*, IV.i.125-6). But for Elizabethan writers a theory of vicegerency is not incompatible with an elective monarchy. This apparent contradiction is evident in a passage from the 1563 edition of *The Mirror for Magistrates* where the contemporary editor, William Baldwin, asserts in an address to the reader both that kings are God's deputies on earth and also that they may be appointed by common consent of the people.

Whatsoever man, woman, or child, is by the consent of the whole realm established in the royal seat, so it have not been injuriously procured by rigour of sword and open force, but quietly by title, either of inheritance, succession, lawful bequest, common consent, or election, is undoubtedly chosen by God to be his deputy; and whosoever resisteth any such, resisteth against God himself, and is a rank traitor and rebel. All resist that wilfully break any law, not being against God's law, made by common consent for the wealth of the realm, and commanded to be kept by the authority of the prince; or that deny to pay such duties, as by consent of the high court of parliament, are appointed to the prince for the defence and preservation of the realm.

William Baldwin 'To the Reader', The Mirror for
Magistrates (1563), pp.420-1.

What is interesting about Baldwin's statement is its ambiguity. Although he claims that resistance is always wrong, his definition of kingship allows for precisely the sort of situation in which Bolingbroke and Richmond acquired the title. In effect he is making the pragmatic observation that the consent of the people, and therefore their willing obedience, is a more important qualification for kingship than hereditary title. The point is made in a negative form in the second act of *Richard II* where the king not only shows a total disregard for the feelings and opinions of his peers, but violates the very principle of heredity he so passionately advocates.

> *North.* My liege, old Gaunt commends him to your
> Majesty.
> *K. Rich.* What savs he?
> *North.*   Nay, nothing; all is said.
> His tongue is now a stringless instrument;
> Words, life, and all, old Lancaster hath spent.
> *York.* Be York the next that must be bankrupt so!
> Though death be poor, it ends a mortal woe.
> *K. Rich.* The ripest fruit first falls, and so doth he;
> His time is spent our pilgrimage must be.
> So much for that. Now for our Irish wars.
> We must supplant those rough rug-headed kerns,
> Which live like venom where no venom else
> But only they have privilege to live.
> And for these great affairs do ask some charge,
> Towards our assistance we do seize to us
> The plate, coin, revenues, and moveables
> Whereof our uncle Gaunt did stand possess'd.
> *York.* How long shall I be patient? Ah, how long
> Shall tender duty make me suffer wrong?
> Not Gloucester's death, nor Hereford's banishment,
> Nor Gaunt's rebukes, nor England's private wrongs,
> Nor the prevention of poor Bolingbroke
> About his marriage, nor my own disgrace,

Have ever made me sour my patient cheek
Or bend one wrinkle on my sovereign's face.
I am the last of noble Edward's sons,
Of whom thy father, Prince of Wales, was first.
In war was never lion rag'd more fierce,
In peace was never gentle lamb more mild,
Than was that young and princely gentleman.
His face thou hast, for even so look'd he,
Accomplish'd with the number of thy hours;
But when he frown'd, it was against the French
And not against his friends. His noble hand
Did win what he did spend, and spent not that
Which his triumphant father's hand had won.
His hands were guilty of no kindred blood,
But bloody with the enemies of his kin.
O Richard! York is too far gone with grief,
Or else he never would compare between–
K. Rich. Why, uncle what's the matter?
York.   O my liege,
Pardon me, if you please; if not, I, pleas'd
Not to be pardoned, am content withal.
Seek you to seize and gripe into your hands
The royalties and rights of banish'd Hereford?
Is not Gaunt dead? and doth not Hereford live?
Was not Gaunt just? and is not Harry true?
Did not the one deserve to have an heir?
Is not his heir a well-deserving son?
Take Hereford's rights away, and take from Time
His charters and his customary rights;
Let not to-morrow then ensue to-day;
Be not thyself–for how art thou a king
But by fair sequence and succession?
Now, afore God–God forbid I say true!–
If you do wrongfully seize Hereford's rights,
Call in the letters patents that he hath
By his attorneys-general to sue
His livery, and deny his off'red homage,
You pluck a thousand dangers on your head,
You lose a thousand well-disposed hearts,
And prick my tender patience to those thoughts
Which honour and allegiance cannot think.

> *K. Rich.* Think what you will, we seize into our
>   hands
> His plate, his goods, his money, and his lands.
> *York.* I'll not be by the while. My liege, farewell.
> What will ensue hereof there's none can tell;
> But by bad courses may be understood
> That their events can never fall out good.
>
> > *Richard II*,II.i.147-214.

As foreign threats to the security of the monarchy diminished, particularly after the defeat of the Spanish Armada in 1588, its doctrine of absolute obedience came to be viewed with increasing scepticism by radical minorities. The establishment responded to this criticism with even more vigorous assertions of the sacrosanctity of kings. But while the debate on the right to resist became increasingly polarised in the final years of the century, moderate writers continued to echo Sir Thomas Smith's cautious pragmatism, warning of the dangers of rebellion, yet refusing unequivocally to condemn it.

> When the commonwealth is evil governed by an evil ruler and unjust, if the laws be made, as most like they be always to maintain that estate, the question remaineth whether the obedience of them be just, and the disobedience wrong; the profit and conservation of that estate right and justice, or the dissolution; and whether a good and upright man and lover of his country ought to maintain and obey them, or to seek by all means to dissolve and abolish them. Great and haughty courages hath taken one part, and this made Dion to rise against Dionysius; and Thrasibulus against the thirty tyrants; Brutus and Cassius against Caesar; and hath been cause of many commotions in commonwealths, whereof the judgement of the common people is according to the event and success; of them which be learned, according to the purpose of the doers, and the estate of the time then present. Certain it is that it is always a doubtful and hazardous matter to meddle with the changing of the laws and government, or to disobey the orders of the rule or

government, which a man doth find already established.

Sir Thomas Smith, *De Republica Anglorum*, pp.51-2.

Although it would be unwise to try to identify plays as complex and subtle as Shakespeare's histories with the views of any single contemporary figure, it is clear that Shakespeare has much sympathy with Sir Thomas Smith's definition of a king, viz, one 'who by succession or election commeth with the good will of the people to that government' (p.53). What we find in Shakespeare is not the didactic assertion of an 'orthodox' doctrine of absolute obedience to kingly authority, but a recognition, first of the horrors of civil war, and second, of the fact that in practice a usurper of ability may contribute more to social harmony than an irresponsible king with impeccable hereditary credentials.

5 Providence and History

In the 16th-century debate on rebellion great emphasis was placed by conservative writers on the sin of disobedience. Appealing to St Paul's Epistle to the Romans (13:1-7) the 1570 *Homilie Agaynst Disobedience* claimed that 'Whosoever resisteth the power [of princes] resisteth the ordinance of God'. It argued not only 'that God doth give princes wisdom, great power, and authority', but also 'that God defendeth them against their enemies horribly' (Sigs Aii^v-Aiii). It is not difficult to find dramatic expression of such views in the histories, though of course we should not assume that they are necessarily Shakespeare's own. In his speech to the rebel peers at Flint Castle Richard II predicts that their insurrection will be punished by God.

> To watch the fearful bending of thy knee,
> Because we thought ourself thy lawful king;
> And if we be, how dare thy joints forget
> To pay their awful duty to our presence?
> If we be not, show us the hand of God
> That hath dismiss'd us from our stewardship;
> For well we know no hand of blood and bone
> Can gripe the sacred handle of our sceptre,
> Unless he do profane, steal, or usurp.
> And though you think that all, as you have done,
> Have torn their souls by turning them from us,
> And we are barren and bereft of friends,
> Yet know–my master, God omnipotent,
> Is mustering in his clouds on our behalf
> Armies of pestilence; and they shall strike
> Your children yet unborn and unbegot,
> That lift your vassal hand against my head
> And threat the glory of my precious crown.
> Tell Bolingbroke, for yon methinks he stands,
> That every stride he makes upon my land

Is dangerous treason; he is come to open
The purple testament of bleeding war;
But ere the crown he looks for live in peace,
Ten thousand bloody crowns of mothers' sons
Shall ill become the flower of England's face,
Change the complexion of her maid-pale peace
To scarlet indignation, and bedew
Her pastor's grass with faithful English blood.

Richard II,III.iii.72-100.

It is Richard's belief in an avenging deity which allows him with such confidence to predict the fall of the Lancasters. Insofar as Bolingbroke's rebellion was to lead to the Wars of the Roses, Richard's prediction of future bloodshed is accurate. However, there is deep irony in his appeal to the traditional idea of the king as 'pastor of the people' (Lipsius, *Sixe Bookes of Politickes*, p.23). In the light of his policy of 'farming' the kingdom for his own profit (I.iv.45), Richard's pastoral mataphor suggests, not the idea of God's special protection, but prophecy of another kind. In the words of Ezekiel: 'Woe be to the shepherds ... that do feed themselves! Should not the shepherds feed the flocks? Ye eat the fat, and ye clothe you with the wool, ye kill them that are fed: but ye feed not the flock ... with force and with cruelty have ye ruled them. And they are scattered because there is no shepherd' (Ezekiel 34:2-5).

The idea, based on the second commandment of the Decalogue (Deuteronomy 5:9-10), that God takes an active interest in human affairs, intervening to protect the good and punish the wicked, had always been an important element in the Christian view of history. With the Reformation a new stress was laid on the doctrine of special providence. Fundamental to Reformation theology is the notion of predestination. The elect are guaranteed salvation, not through their own efforts, but by God's free grace, preordained from the beginning of time. It is because he wishes to emphasise man's complete dependence on divine grace that Calvin insists that God is responsible, not just for the general direction of the world, but for every eventuality.

When the sense of the flesh hath once set before it the power of God in the very creation, it resteth there, and when it proceedeth furthest of all, it doth nothing but weigh and consider the wisdom, power, and goodness of the workman in making such a piece of work (which things do of themselves offer and thrust themselves in sight of men whether they will or no) and a certain general doing in preserving and governing the same, upon which dependeth the power of moving. Finally it thinketh that the lively force at the beginning put into all things by God, doth suffice to sustain them. But faith ought to pierce deeper, that is to say, whom he hath learned to be the creator of all things, by and by to gather that the same is the perpetual governor and preserver of them; and that not by stirring with an universal motion as well the whole frame of the world, as all the parts thereof, but by sustaining, cherishing and caring for, with singular providence every one of those things that He hath created even to the least sparrow . . . .

That this difference may the better appear, it is to be known, that the providence of God, such as it is taught in the scripture, is in comparison set as contrary to fortune and chances that happen by adventure. Now forasmuch as it hath been commonly believed in all ages, and the same opinion is at this day also in a manner in all men, that all things happen by fortune, it is certain, that that which ought to have been believed concerning providence, is by that wrong opinion not only darkened but also in manner buried. If a man light among thieves or wild beasts; if by wind suddenly rising he suffer shipwreck on the sea; if he be killed with the fall of a house or of a tree; if another wandering in desert places find remedy for his poverty; if having been tossed with the waves, he attain to the haven; if miraculously he escape but a finger breadth from death, all these chances as well of prosperity as of adversity the reason of the flesh doth ascribe to fortune. But whosoever is taught by the mouth of Christ, that all the hairs of his head are numbered, will seek for a cause further off, and will

firmly believe that all chances are governed by the
secret counsel of God . . . .

And truly God doth claim and will have us give
unto Him an almightiness, not such as the sophists do
imagine, vain, idle, and as it were sleeping, but
waking, effectual, working and busied in continual
doing. Nor such a one as is only a general beginning
of a confused motion, as if he would command a river
to flow by his appointed channels, but such a one as is
bent and ready at all His particular movings. For He
is therefore called almighty, not because He can do
and yet sitteth still and doth nothing, or by general
instinct only continueth the order of nature that He
hath before appointed; but because He, governing
both heaven and earth by His providence, so ordereth
all things that nothing chanceth but by His advised
purpose . . . .
Therefore let the readers learn, that providence is
called that, not wherewith God idly beholdeth from
heaven what is done in the world, but wherewith as
guiding the stern He setteth and ordereth all things
that come to pass.

Jean Calvin, *The Institution of Christian Religion,*
fols 45-7.

The role played by providence in human affairs is a
preoccupation of many of Shakespeare's characters. Hamlet,
for example, makes specific reference to the doctrine of
special providence before his fatal duel with Laertes – though
when Shakespeare has Hamlet speak of God's care for all his
creatures he is no doubt thinking, not of Calvin, but of St
Matthew (10:29).

> *Lord.* The Queen desires you to use some gentle
> entertainment to Laertes before you fall to play.
> *Ham.* She well instructs me, [*Exit Lord.*]
> *Hor.* You will lose this wager, my lord.
> *Ham.* I do not think so; since he went into France I
> have been in continual practice. I shall win at the
> odds. But thou wouldst not think how ill all's here
> about my heart; but it is no matter.

Hor. Nay, good my lord–
Ham. It is but foolery; but it is such a kind of
gain-giving as would perhaps trouble a woman,
Hor. If your mind dislike anything, obey it. I will
forestall their repair hither, and say you are not fit.
Ham. Not a whit, we defy augury: there is a special
providence in the fall of a sparrow. If it be now, 'tis
not to come; if it be not to come, it will be now; if it
be not now, yet it will come–the readiness is all. Since
no man owes of aught he leaves, what is't to leave
betimes? Let be.

Hamlet, V.ii.198-215.

How we are to interpret such expressions of belief in special providence is not easy to say. In Hamlet's case this passive fatalism is in dramatic contrast to his earlier sense of a personal mission to set the world to rights. Such extreme attitudes are in keeping with what we see of his volatile temperament; they suggest that, in failing to live up to his own ideal of rational stoicism, he is allowing himself to become a hostage to fortune in precisely the way he had foreseen (III.ii.66-9).

In other plays the idea of providence is treated with less scepticism. In *Macbeth*, the only tragedy of Shakespeare's maturity in which the hero is a self-confessed villain, an act of regicide provokes unmistakable signs of divine anger.

Old Man. Threescore and ten I can remember well;
Within the volume of which time I have seen
Hours dreadful and things strange; but this sore night
Hath trifled former knowings.
Ross.   Ah, good father,
Thou seest, the heavens, as troubled with man's act,
Threatens his bloody stage. By th' clock 'tis day,
And yet dark night strangles the travelling lamp.
Is't night's predominance, or the day's shame,
That darkness does the face of earth entomb,
When living light should kiss it?
Old M.   'Tis unnatural,
Even like the deed that's done. On Tuesday last,
A falcon, tow'ring in her pride of place,

Was by a mousing owl hawk'd at and kill'd.
Ross. And Duncan's horses–a thing most strange and
   certain–
Beauteous and swift, the minions of their race,
Turn'd wilde in nature, broke their stalls, flung out,
Contending 'gainst obedience, as they would make
War with mankind.
Old M.   'Tis said they eat each other.
Ross. They did so; to the amazement of mine eyes,
That look'd upon't.

Macbeth, II.iv.1-20.

With its emphasis on God's active involvement in the affairs of the world Calvinism had the effect of encouraging men to look for signs of God's anger or approval in natural phenomena. In *Macbeth* there is nothing to suggest that Ross and the Old Man are particularly credulous or superstitious: indeed the whole play would seem to confirm their sense of heaven's outrage at the murder of Duncan. But belief in divine intervention is susceptible to exaggeration or abuse. Bishop Ponet's providentialist interpretation of such phenomena as unnatural births or comets in his *A Short Treatise of Politic Power* must be seen as part of a campaign by the Marian exiles to remove a Catholic queen from the English throne.

> There was never great misery, destruction, plague or visitation of God, that came on any nation, city or country, which as they be in deed, so may they justly be called wounds, but be sent of God for sin, and be not suddenly laid on the people, but are before prophesied and declared by the prophets and ministers of God's word, or by some revelations, wonders, monsters in the earth or tokens and signs in the element.
>
> For as God is most just, and will not fail to punish sin, so is He most merciful, and wills not the death of sinners, but rather that they should turn to Him and live; and therefore beforehand giveth them warning what shall follow if in time they repent not, as by the histories of all ages it doth appear. And none of these

admonitions have ye lacked, countrymen.

For the preachers and ministers of God's word, in the time of the godly Josias, King Edward IV, preached and prophesied unto you what miseries and plagues should certainly come to you: the food of God's word to be clean taken away from you, famine of the body, pestilence, wars, the loss of your goods, the deflowering and ravishing of your wives and daughters before your eyes, the captivity of your bodies, and wives and children; the subversion of the policy and state of the realm; that a strange king and strange people (not only in country, but also in conditions and manners in respect of your own) should reign and rule by force over you, if ye in time repented you not of your wickedness, amended your lives, and called to God for mercy.

But then ye passed nothing on it, but as the Jews being drowned in sin, mocked and scorned and murdered the prophets of God which long before prophesied unto them their captivities and utter destruction, so ye laughed and jested at your preachers' words, nothing regarding the threats of God, but contemning them, yea increasing in your wickedness, and now at length murdering most cruelly the ministers of God.

And seeing words of warning took no place with you, God for his loving mercy hath warned you also by monstrous marvels on the earth, and horrible wonders in the element, to put you beside all manner of excuses. And what wonderful monsters have there now lately been in England? And what celestial signs most horrible? A child born beside Oxford in the year 1552 with two heads and two parts of two evil shaped bodies joined in one. A child born at Coventry in the year 1555 without arms or legs. A child born at Fulham in London even now this year, with a great head, evil shaped, the arms with bags hanging out at the elbows and heels, and feet lame. A child new born at London forthwith speaking as a prophet and messenger of God. An horrible comet this year, besides diverse eclipses, which follow. But what were these? Only bare signs? No certainly, they do and must signify the great wrath and indignation of God.

John Ponet, *A Short Treatise of Politic Power*,
Sigs Kii^v-Kiii^v.

When providentialism is taken to such literal extremes there is little to choose between Ponet's conception of divine justice and the superstitious determinism of a character like Gloucester in *King Lear*.

> *Glo.* These late eclipses in the sun and moon portend no good to us. Though the wisdom of nature can reason it thus and thus, yet nature finds itself scourg'd by the sequent effects: love cools, friendship falls off, brothers divide; in cities, mutinies; in countries, discord; in palaces, treason; and the bond crack'd 'twixt son and father. This villain of mine comes under the prediction: there's son against father. The King falls from bias of nature: there's father against child. We have seen the best of our time: machinations, hollowness, treachery, and all ruinous disorders, follow us disquietly to our graves. Find out this villain, Edmund; it shall lose thee nothing; do it carefully. And the noble and true-hearted Kent banish'd! His offence, honesty! 'Tis strange. [*Exit.*]
> *Edm.* This is the excellent foppery of the world, that, when we are sick in fortune, often the surfeits of our own behaviour, we make guilty of our disasters the sun, the moon, and stars; as if we were villains on necessity; fools by heavenly compulsion; knaves, thieves, and teachers, by spherical predominance; drunkards, liars, and adulterers, by an enforc'd obedience of planetary influence; and all that we are evil in, by a divine thrusting on–an admirable evasion of whoremaster man, to lay his goatish disposition on the charge of a star! My father compounded with my mother under the Dragon's tail, and my nativity was under Ursa Major, so that it follows I am rough and lecherous. Fut, I should have been that I am, had the maidenliest star in the firmament twinkled on my bastardizing. . . .

O, these eclipses do portend these divisions!
fa, sol, la, mi

King Lear, I.ii.99-131.

Gloucester's naive belief in the influence of the stars and Edmund's sceptical response form part of an unresolved debate in *King Lear* on the role of the gods in human affairs.

From the variety of ways in which providence is treated in the histories and tragedies it is clear that Shakespeare is using it as a dramatic device, sometimes, as in *Macbeth*, to imply the existence of a beneficient natural order, and sometimes to satirise credulity, but usually appeals to providence form part of a dialectic in which opposing views are contrasted. Certainly this is true of the English history plays where Shakespeare's characters tend to interpret events in the light of their own interests. In this respect the plays reflect their sources.

For many years after Tillyard published his book on the histories it was widely accepted that Shakespeare's chronicle sources saw the Wars of the Roses as God's punishment for the crime committed by Henry Bolingbroke in deposing a reigning monarch. This ancestral curse was thought to be finally expiated when Henry Tudor defeated the tyrannical Richard III and united the two royal houses through his marriage to Elizabeth of York. In doing so Henry, who was believed to be descended from the ancient Celtic dynasty, claimed to be fulfilling a prophecy that King Arthur would return to unite a divided nation and restore the legendary Golden Age. This so-called 'Tudor Myth' is a composite theory consisting of a number of disparate elements. Although evidence for some of these may be found in contemporary writings, it would be incorrect to say that the myth as a whole represented the standard Elizabethan view of English history.

The idea that Henry VII was providentially appointed to bring peace to a divided nation was welcomed for its obvious political value by his son and granddaughter. In the following passage from *Euphues and His England* John Lyly presents a popular Elizabethan version of recent history.

There were for a long time civil wars in this country, by reason of several claims to the crown, between the two famous and noble houses of Lancaster and York, either of them pretending to be of the royal blood, which caused them both to spend their vital blood. These jars continued long, not without great loss, both to the nobility and commonality, who joining not in one, but divers parts, turned the realm to great ruin, having almost destroyed their country before they could anoint a king.

But the living God who was loath to oppress England, at last began to repress injuries, and to give an end by mercy, to those that could find no end of malice, nor look for any end of mischief. So tender a care hath He always had of that England, as of a new Israel, his chosen and peculiar people.

This peace began by a marriage solemnised by God's special providence, between Henry Earl of Richmond heir of the house of Lancaster, and Elizabeth daughter to Edward IV, the undoubted issue and heir of the house of York, whereby (as they term it) the red rose and the white were united and joined together. Out of these roses sprang two noble buds, Prince Arthur and Henry, the eldest dying without issue, the other of most famous memory, leaving behind him three children, Prince Edward, the Lady Mary, the Lady Elizabeth. King Edward lived not long, which could never for that realm have lived too long, but sharp frosts bite forward springs; easterly winds blasteth towardly blossoms, cruel death spareth not those which we ourselves living cannot spare.

The elder sister, the Princess Mary, succeeded as next heir to the crown, and as it chanced next heir to the grave, touching whose life, I can say little because I was scarce borne, and what others say, of me shall be forborn.

This queen being deceased, Elizabeth being of the age of twenty two years, of more beauty than honour, and yet of more honour than any earthly creature, was called from a prisoner to be a prince, from the castle to the crown, from the fear of losing her head, to be supreme head.

But being now placed in the seat royal, she first of all established religion, banished popery, advanced the word, that before was so much defaced, who having in her hand the sword to revenge, used rather bountifully to reward, being as far from rigour when she might have killed, as her enemies were from honesty when they could not; giving a general pardon, when she had cause to use particular punishments; preferring the name of pity before the remembrance of perils; thinking no revenge more princely, than to spare when she might spill, to stay when she might strike, to proffer to save with mercy, when she might have destroyed with justice.

John Lyly, *Eupheus and His England* (1580), *The Complete Works of John Lyly*, pp.205-7.

At a time when anti-court satire had begun to flourish and writers were adopting increasingly polarised political positions, Shakespeare avoided controversy, subtly reflecting, but not endorsing the more extreme views. One exception is Cranmer's sentimental vision of the future Queen Elizabeth in *Henry VIII*, written, possibly in collaboration with John Fletcher, some ten years after Elizabeth's death.

This royal infant–heaven still move about her!–
Though in her cradle, yet now promises
Upon this land a thousand thousand blessings,
Which time shall bring to ripeness. She shall be–
But few now living can behold that goodness–
A pattern to all princes living with her,
And all that shall succeed. Saba was never
More covetous of wisdom and fair virtue
Than this pure soul shall be. All princely graces
That mould up such a mighty piece as this is,
With all the virtues that attend the good,
Shall still be doubled on her. Truth shall nurse her.
Holy and heavenly thoughts still counsel her;
She shall be lov'd and fear'd. Her own shall bless her:
Her foes shake like a field of beaten corn,

And hang their heads with sorrow. Good grows with
   her;
In her days every man shall eat in safety
Under his own vine what he plants, and sing
The merry songs of peace to all his neighbours.
God shall be truly known; and those about her
From her shall read the perfect ways of honour,
And by those claim their greatness, not by blood.

*   *   *

She shall be, to the happiness of England,
An aged princess; many days shall see her,
And yet no day without a deed to crown it.
Would I had known no more! But she must die–
She must, the saints must have her–yet a virgin;
A most unspotted lily shall she pass
To th' ground, and all the world shall mourn her.

Henry VIII, V.v.17-38; 56-62.

If there was widespread popular acceptance of the idea that
Elizabeth, as head of a Reformation state, was in some sense
the instrument of providence, there is certainly no proof that
the Wars of the Roses were universally regarded by Tudor
and Elizabethan writers as the consequence of an ancestral
curse incurred by Henry Bolingbroke's rebellion; or indeed
that the idea of divine vengeance was 'a staple of their time'
(R.R. Reed Jr, *Crime and God's Punishment in Shakespeare*,
p.6). In an important study of 15th- and 16th-century
chronicles H.A. Kelly has shown that providential interpretations of these events tended to reflect their authors' political
allegiances, with Lancastrian sympathisers representing
Richard's overthrow as divine retribution for his sins and
Yorkists portraying it as a crime against God. An illustration
of the confusion created by these competing views may be
seen in the revised edition of Holinshed's *Chronicles* (the
edition used by Shakespeare) where, as a result of the
indiscriminate interpolations of its editors, both Lancastrian
and Yorkist interpretations of Richard's deposition are
offered, the latter flatly contradicting the former.

He [Richard] was prodigal, ambitious, and much given to the pleasure of the body. He kept the greatest port, and maintained the most plentiful house that ever any king in England did either before his time or since. For there resorted daily to his court above ten thousand persons that had meat and drink there allowed them. In his kitchen there were three hundred servitors, and every other office was furnished after the like rate. Of ladies, chamberers, and launderers, there were above three hundred at the least. And in gorgious and costly apparel they exceeded all measure, not one of them that kept within the bounds of his degree. Yeomen and grooms were clothed in silks, with cloth of grain [red dye] and scarlet, over-sumptuous ye may be sure for their estates. And this vanity was not only used in the court in those days, but also other people abroad in the towns and countries, had their garments cut far otherwise than had been accustomed before his days, with embroideries, rich furs, and goldsmiths' work, and every day there was devising of new fashions, to the great hinderance and decay of the commonwealth.

Moreover, such were preferred to bishoprics, and other ecclesiastical livings, as neither could teach or preach, nor knew anything of the scripture of God, but only to call for their tithes and duties; so that they were most unworthy the name of bishops, being lewd and most vain persons disguised in bishops' apparel. Furthermore, there reigned abundantly the filthy sin of lechery and fornication, with abominable adultery, specially in the king, but most chiefly in the prelacy, whereby the whole realm by such their evil example, was so infected, that the wrath of God was daily provoked to vengeance for the sins of the prince and his people. How then could it continue prosperously with this king? Against whom for the foul enormities wherewith his life was defamed, the wrath of God was whetted and took so sharp an edge, that the same did shred him off the scepter of his kingdom, and gave him a full cup of affliction to drink, as he had done to other kings his predecessors, by whose example he might have taken warning. For it is an heavy case when God thundereth out his real arguments either upon prince or people.

Thus have ye heard what writers do report touching the state of the time and doings of this king. But if I may boldly say what I think: he was a prince the most unthankfully used of his subjects, of any one of whom ye shall lightly read. For although (through the frailty of youth) he demeaned himself more dissolutely than seemed convenient for his royal estate, and made choice of such counsellors as were not favoured of the people, whereby he was the less favoured himself, yet in no king's days were the commons in greater wealth, if they could have perceived their happy state; neither in any other time were the nobles and gentlemen more cherished, nor churchmen less wronged. But such was their ingratitude towards their bountiful and loving sovereign, that those whom he had chiefly advanced, were readiest to control him, for that they might not rule all things at their will, and remove from him such as they misliked, and place in their rooms whom they thought good, and that rather by strong hand, than by gentle and courteous means, which stirred such malice betwixt him and them, till at length it could not be assuaged without peril of destruction to them both.

The Duke of Gloucester, chief instrument of this mischief, to what end he came ye have heard. And although his nephew the Duke of Hereford took upon him to revenge his death, yet wanted he moderation and loyalty in his doings, for the which both he himself and his lineal race were scourged afterwards, as a due punishment unto rebellious subjects.

Raphael Holinshed, *Chronicles of England, Scotland, and Ireland*, vol. II, p.868-9.

It is against the reality of this complex historical debate that the Yorkist prophecies of a character like the Bishop of Carlisle must be seen.

York. Great Duke of Lancaster, I come to thee
From plume-pluck'd Richard, who with willing soul
Adopts thee heir, and his high sceptre yields
To the possession of thy royal hand.
Ascend his throne, descending now from him—
And long live Henry, fourth of that name!
Boling. In God's name, I'll ascend the regal throne.
Car. Marry, God forbid!
Worst in this royal presence may I speak,
Yet best beseeming me to speak the truth.
Would God that any in this noble presence
Were enough noble to be upright judge
Of noble Richard! Then true noblesse would
Learn him forbearance from so foul a wrong.
What subject can give sentence on his king?
And who sits here that is not Richard's subject?
Thieves are not judg'd but they are by to hear,
Although apparent guilt be seen in them;
And shall the figure of God's majesty,
His captain, steward, deputy elect,
Anointed, crowned, planted many years,
Be judg'd by subject and inferior breath,
And he himself not present? O, forfend it, God,
That in a Christian climate souls refin'd
Should show so heinous, black, obscene a deed!
I speak to subjects, and a subject speaks,
Stirr'd up by God, thus boldly for his king.
My Lord of Hereford here, whom you call king,
Is a foul traitor to proud Hereford's king;
And if you crown him, let me prophesy—
The blood of English shall manure the ground,
And future ages groan for this foul act;
Peace shall go sleep with Turks and infidels,
And in this seat of peace tumultuous wars
Shall kin with kin and kind with kind confound;
Disorder, horror, fear and mutiny,
Shall here inhabit, and this land be call'd
The field of Golgotha and dead men's skulls.
O, if you raise this house against this house,
It will the woefullest division prove
That ever fell upon this cursed earth.

Prevent it, resist it, let it not be so,
Lest child, child's children, cry against you woe.

Richard II, IV.i.107-149.

Prophecy is an effective dramatic device and is often used by Shakespeare to create suspense. The fact that Carlisle's prediction proves true does not confirm that God is intervening on the side of York: civil war might well have been anticipated on empirical grounds, as it is in *Julius Caesar* when, following the murder of Caesar, Mark Antony prophesies insurrection in Rome.

Over thy wounds now do I prophesy—
Which like dumb mouths do ope their ruby lips
To beg the voice and utterance of my tongue—
A curse shall light upon the limbs of men;
Domestic fury and fierce civil strife
Shall cumber all the parts of Italy;
Blood and destruction shall be so in use,
And dreadful objects so familiar,
That mothers shall but smile when they behold
Their infants quartered with the hands of war,
All pity chok'd with custom of fell deeds;
And Caesar's spirit, ranging for revenge,
With Até by his side come hot from hell,
Shall in these confines with a monarch's voice
Cry 'Havoc!' and let slip the dogs of war,
That this foul deed shall smell above the earth
With carrion men, groaning for burial.

Julius Caesar, III.i.260-276.

By Shakespeare's time historians had begun increasingly to look for meaning in history, not in God's will, but in human character. With their emphasis on the moral as opposed to the political value of history and their demonstration of man's total ignorance of his destiny, Shakespeare's chronicle sources belonged to the past. The sense of the instability of life and the precariousness of high office expressed in Edward Hall's response to Richard II's murder in Pomfret (Pontefract)

Castle are in the medieval *de casibus*[1] tradition.

> After which act [entailing the succession to Boling-
> broke's heirs] passed, he thought never to be by any
> of his subjects molested or troubled. But O Lord,
> what is the mutability of fortune? O God, what is the
> change of worldly safety? O Christ, what stableness
> consisteth in man's provision? Or what firm surety
> hath a prince in his throne and degree? Considering
> this king having the possession of the crown and
> realm, and that in open parliament, agreed to by the
> princes, condescended to by the clerks, ratified by the
> commons, and enacted by the three estates of the
> realm, was when he thought himself surely mortised
> in a firm rock and immovable foundation, suddenly
> with a trembling quicksand and unsteadfast ground
> like to have sunk or been overthrown. For diverse
> lords which were King Richard's friends, outwardly
> dissimuled that which they inwardly conspired and
> determined, to confound this King Henry to whom
> they had both sworn allegiance and done homage, and
> to erect again and set up their old lord and friend King
> Richard II . . . .
> O Lord I would wish that this example, of many
> highly promoted to rule, might be had in memory, the
> which mete and measure their own iniquity and ill
> doings, with force authority and power, to the intent
> that they by these examples should avert their minds
> from ill doings, and such ungodly and execrable
> offences . . . .
> But now was come the time when all the
> confederates and companions of this unhappy
> sedition, had tasted according to their deserts, the
> painful penance of their pleasant pastime, or rather
> pestiferous obstinacy, that an innocent with a nocent
> [criminal], a man unguilty with a guilty, was
> pondered in an egal balance. For poor King Richard
> ignorant of all this conjuration kept in miserable
> captivity, knowing nothing but that he saw in his

[1]From the title of Boccaccio's *De casibus virorum illustrium* (c.1360). For the Middle Ages tragedy was epitomised by the fall of an eminent person from felicity to misfortune.

chamber, was by King Henry adjudged to die, because that he being singed and tickled with the last crafty policy of his enemies, would deliver himself out of all inward fear and discord, and clean put away the very ground whereof such fruits of displeasure might by any wise be attempted against him, so that no man hereafter should either feign or resemble to represent the person of King Richard. Wherefore some say he commanded, others talk that he condescended, many write that he knew not till it was done and then it confirmed. But howsoever it was, King Richard died of a violent death without any infection or natural disease of the body.

Edward Hall, *Hall's Chronicle* (1548), pp.15; 19.

As humanism came to influence every aspect of European thought, historians turned to classical antiquity for their models. Although the medieval attempt to encompass the whole course of human history in terms of a single apocalyptic vision can still be seen in books like Sir Walter Raleigh's vast and fragmentary *History of the World* (1614), the new historians concerned themselves not with man's eternal salvation, but with the more immediate problem of his political survival. Elements of the new interest in human behaviour may sometimes be seen in writers like Hall and Holinshed and their mentor Polydore Vergil. But it was not until the influence of Machiavelli and Guicciardini made itself felt that historians began seriously to develop the political aspects of their material. Jaques Amyot's preface to his French translation of Plutarch's *Lives of the Noble Grecians and Romans* contains an eloquent defence of the new pragmatic approach to history (Shakespeare's *Plutarch* was a re-translation of this edition by Sir Thomas North in 1579).

[History] is a certain rule and instruction, which by examples past, teacheth us to judge of things present, and to foresee things to come, so as we may know what to like of, and what to follow; what to mislike, and what to eschew. It is a picture, which (as it were in a table) setteth before our eyes the things worthy of remembrance that have been done in old times by mighty nations, noble kings and princes, wise governors, valiant captains, and persons renowned for some notable quality, representing unto us the manners of strange nations, the laws and customs of old time, the particular affairs of men, their consultations and enterprises, the means that they have used to compass them withal, and their demeaning of themselves when they were come to the highest, or thrown down to the lowest degree of state. So as it is not possible for any case to rise either in peace or war, in public or private affairs, but that the person which shall have diligently read, well conceived, and thoroughly remembered histories, shall find matter in them whereas to take light, and counsel whereby to resolve himself to take a part, or to give advice unto others, how to choose in doubtful and dangerous cases that which may be for their most profit, and in time to find out to what point the matter will come if it be well handled; and how to moderate himself in prosperity, and how to cheer up and bear himself in adversity. These things it doth with much greater grace, efficacy, and speed, than the books of moral philosophy do, forasmuch as examples are of more force to move and instruct, than are the arguments and proofs of reason, or their precise precepts, because examples be the very forms of our deeds, and accompanied with all circumstances . . . .

To be short, it may be truly said, that the reading of histories is the school of wisdom, to fashion men's understanding, by considering advisedly the state of the world that is past, and by marking diligently by what laws, manners, and discipline, empires, kingdoms and dominions, have in old time been established, and afterwards maintained and increased; or contrariwise changed, diminished, and overthrown.

Jaques Amyot, Preface to Plutarch's *Lives of the Noble Grecians and Romans* (1559, trans. 1579), vol. I, pp.10-12.

It is a similar view of history which Warwick puts to
Henry IV in response to the king's pessimistic recollection of
the prophecies that were made at the time of his coronation.

> *King.* O God! that one might read the book of fate,
> And see the revolution of the times
> Make mountains level, and the continent,
> Weary of solid firmness, melt itself
> Into the sea; and other times to see
> The beachy girdle of the ocean
> Too wide for Neptune's hips; how chances mock,
> And changes fill the cup of alteration
> With divers liquors! O, if this were seen,
> The happiest youth, viewing his progress through,
> What perils past, what crosses to ensue,
> Would shut the book and sit him down and die.
> 'Tis not ten years gone
> Since Richard and Northumberland, great friends,
> Did feast together, and in two years after
> Were they at wars. It is but eight years since
> This Percy was the man nearest my soul;
> Who like a brother toil'd in my affairs
> And laid his love and life under my foot;
> Yea, for my sake, even to the eyes of Richard
> Gave him defiance. But which of you was by–
> [*To Warwick*] You cousin Nevil, as I may remember–
> When Richard, with his eyes brim full of tears,
> Then check'd and rated by Northumberland,
> Did speak these words, now prov'd a prophecy?
> 'Northumberland, thou ladder by the which
> My cousin Bolingbroke ascends my throne'–
> Though then, God knows, I had no such intent
> But that necessity so bow'd the state
> That I and greatness were compell'd to kiss–
> 'The time shall come' –thus did he follow it–
> 'The time will come that foul sin, gathering head,
> Shall break into corruption' so went on,
> Foretelling this same time's condition
> And the division of our amity.
> *War.* There is a history in all men's lives,
> Figuring the natures of the times deceas'd;

The which observ'd, a man may prophesy
With a near aim, of the main chance of things
As yet not come to life, who in their seeds
And weak beginning lie intreasured.
Such things become the hatch and brood of time;
And by the necessary form of this,
King Richard might create a perfect guess
That great Northumberland, then false to him,
Would of that seed grow to a greater falseness;
Which should not find a ground to root upon
Unless on you.

2 Henry IV, III.i.45–92.

It is clear from this exchange that Shakespeare is aware of the limitations of the old historiography. However, this is not to say that he denies the role of providence in history. While the new historians interested themselves primarily in the way events were determined by human actions, they took it for granted that providence was the ultimate cause of all happenings. Thus when the English historian Richard Knolles, writing in the early years of the 17th century, analyses the causes of the extraordinary success of the Turkish Empire he speaks first of God's will, second of the unpredictability of fortune and third of the human factors involved.

> If you consider the beginning, progress, and perpetual felicity of this the Ottoman Empire, there is in this world nothing more admirable or strange; if the greatness and lustre thereof, nothing more magnificent or glorious; if the power and strength thereof, nothing more dreadful or dangerous, which wondering at nothing but at the beauty of itself, and drunk with the pleasant wine of perpetual felicity, holdeth all the rest of the world in scorn, thundering out nothing but still blood and war, with a full persuasion in time to rule over all, prefining [prescribing] unto itself no other limits than the uttermost bounds of the earth from the rising of the sun unto the going down of the same. The causes whereof are many and right lamentable, but for the most part so shut up in the

counsels of the great, as that for me to seek after them, were great folly. Yet amongst the rest, some others there be, so pregnant and manifest, as that the blind world taketh thereof as it were a general knowledge, and may therefore without offence of the wiser sort (as I hope) even in these our nice days be lightly touched. Whereof the first and greatest, is the just and secret judgement of the Almighty, who in justice delivereth into the hands of these merciless miscreants, nation after nation, and kingdom upon kingdom, as unto the most terrible executioners of his dreadful wrath, to be punished for their sins; others in the meanwhile, no less sinful than they, in His mercy enjoying the benefit of a longer time, calling them unto repentance. Then, the uncertainty of worldly things, which subject to perpetual change, cannot long stay in one state, but as the sea is with the wind, so are they in like sort tossed up and down with the continual surges and waves of alteration and change, so that being once grown to their height, they stay not long, but fall again as fast as ever they rise, and so in time come to nothing, as we see the greatest monarchies that ever yet were upon earth have done, their course being run, over whom time now triumpheth, as no doubt at length it shall over this so great a monarchy also, when it shall but then live by fame, as the others now do. Next to these causes from above (without offence be it said) is the small care the Christian princes, especially those that dwelt further off, have had of the common state of the Christian commonwealth, whereof even the very greatest are to account themselves but as the principal members of one and the same body, and have, or ought to have, as sharp a feeling one of another's harms, as hath the head of the wrongs done unto the feet, or rather, as if it were done unto themselves: instead of which Christian compassion and unity, they are so divided among themselves with endless quarrels, partly for questions of religion (never by the sword to be determined), partly for matters touching their own proper state and sovereignty, and that with such

distrust and implacable hatred, that they never could
as yet (although it have been long wished) join their
common forces against the common enemy, but
turning their weapons one upon another (the more to
be lamented) have from time to time weakened
themselves, and opened a way for him to devour them
one after another.

Richard Knolles, *The Generall Historie of the Turkes*
(1603), Sig. Aiv^v.

History for Shakespeare, like Knolles, is a combination of
many factors. Although appeals are frequently made in the
plays both to a pagan and to a Christian heaven, these are
more often than not ironic in their context and cannot be said
either to confirm or deny divine intervention in human
affairs. What chiefly interests Shakespeare is the way men
shape their destinies through their own acts of folly,
self-deception, superstition and, occasionally, astuteness and
foresight.

6   Natural Law

Despite the prevailing conservatism of 16th-century English moral and philosophic thought Elizabethan writers were aware that the traditional theory of cosmos inherited from the ancient world was beginning seriously to be threatened by scientific discoveries and sceptical philosophic inquiry. The problem was not a purely academic one. In basing their defence of monarchy on an analogical argument, writers from both ends of the political spectrum appealed to a theological premise: if the universe was an essentially rational creation in which the same principles of order and degree were repeated on every plane of existence, it followed logically that human society should be governed by a single figure, god-like in his office if not in his person. But if the premise of this argument were shown to be false, then what of its conclusions?

As society came gradually to be seen, not as a divinely sanctioned institution, but as an aggregate of individuals united by no more lofty a principle than self-interest, kingship lost its special sanctity. Radical opinion claimed that, far from owing their monarch a debt of absolute obedience, the people had, in the words of Dryden's Achitophel,

> a right supreme
> To make their kings, for kings are made for them.
> All empire is no more than power in trust
> Which, when resumed, can be no longer just.

> John Dryden, *Absalom and Achitophel* (1681),
> ll.409-412.

Although Shakespeare did not live to see the civil wars which Dryden is alluding to in these lines, the new spirit of pragmatism they manifest was already by the beginning of the 17th century a potent force in European intellectual life. The term which, perhaps better than any other, serves as an index of the ideological transformation of the early years of the 17th

century is natural law. Originally conceived as a system of
duties and mutual obligations, natural law was gradually
coming to mean the exact opposite: the inalienable rights of
free and equal individuals. A classic humanist definition of
natural law is contained in the first chapter of Thomas
Starkey's treatise on the English constitution.

> There is a certain wit and policy by nature given to
> man in every place and country, whereby he is
> inclined to live in civil order according to the dignity
> of his nature; and to perceive the mean how he may
> attain thereto there is furthermore in all men by
> nature (without any other instruction) rooted a
> certain reverence to God, whereby they honour him
> as governor and ruler of all this world. For yet there
> never was nation so rude or blind but for this cause
> they religiously worshipped and honoured the name
> of God.
>   These virtues, and other like, whereby man (of
> nature meek, gentle and full of humanity) is inclined
> and stirred to civil order and loving company, with
> honest behaviour both toward God and man, are by
> the power of nature in the heart of man rooted and
> planted, and by no vain opinion or fancy conceived.
> And though it be so that among all nations many so
> live as they had utterly forgotten the dignity of this
> their nature, and had no such virtues by nature in
> them set and planted, yet among them all few there
> be, or none, which, so living, judge themself to do
> well, but think themself they are slipped and fallen
> from the excellency of their nature, with great and
> continual grudge of conscience inwardly. For they
> have rooted in their hearts a certain rule, ever
> repugning [opposed] to their manner of living, which
> they by negligent incontinence suffer to be corrupt;
> the which rule so certain and so stable is called, of
> philosophers and wise men, the universal and true law
> of nature, which to all nations is common, nothing
> hanging of the opinion and foolish fancy of man.
> Insomuch that if man by corrupt judgement would

esteem virtue as vice, nothing regarding his own dignity, yet virtues, by their own nature, be no less virtues, nor diminished of their excellency, by any such frantic fancy, no more than if all men together would conspire that there were no God, who by that foolish opinion should nothing be diminished of His high majesty; or if they would say that He neither governeth nor ruleth this world, yet their opinion maketh no less His high providence. Wherefore plainly it appeareth that these virtues stand not in the opinion of man, but by the benefit and power of nature in his heart are rooted and planted, inclining him ever to the civil life, according to the excellent dignity of his nature. And this inclination and rule of living, by these virtues stabled and confirmed, is called, as I said, the law of nature, which, though all men follow not, yet all men approve.

Thomas Starkey, *Dialogue Between Reginald Pole and Thomas Lupset*, pp. 30-1.

Revolutionary as some of Starkey's proposals for constitutional reform were, his theory of natural law is traditional. Two fundamental principles are stated in this passage: first, that natural law is common to all nations and independent of time, custom or opinion; and second, that, because this law has been implanted by God in his heart, man has a natural propensity for civilised order. As an immutable system of ethical imperatives, natural law had from the time of Cicero formed the basis of European political thought. What it meant in practice to the 16th century may be seen in the profoundly ironic exchange between Duncan and Macbeth when the king welcomes his trusted general to Forres Castle.

Dun.   O worthiest cousin!
The sin of my ingratitude even now
Was heavy on me. Thou art so far before
That swiftest wing of recompense is slow
To overtake thee. Would thou hadst less deserv'd,
That the proportion both of thanks and payment

Might have been mine! Only I have left to say,
More is thy due than more than all can pay.
Macb. The service and the loyalty I owe,
In doing it, pays itself. Your Highness part
Is to receive our duties; and our duties
Are to your throne and state children and servants,
Which do but what they should by doing everything
Safe toward your love and honour.
Dun.   Welcome hither.
I have begun to plant thee, and will labour
To make thee full of growing. Noble Banquo,
That hast no less deserv'd, nor must be known
No less to have done so, let me infold thee
And hold thee to my heart.
Ban.   There if I grow,
The harvest is your own.
Dun.   My plenteous joys,
Wanton in fulness, seek to hide themselves
In drops of sorrow.

Macbeth, I.iv.14-35.

The key words of Macbeth's speech are 'service', 'loyalty', 'duty', 'love' and 'honour'. They are carefully chosen, for they sum up with great precision the reciprocal bond which it was believed should exist between king and subject. That the terms of this relationship are not arbitrary, but as natural as the cycle of time itself is implied in the metaphors of planting, tending and reaping of crops in Duncan's and Banquo's responses. The image of society they evoke is one of men and women united in loving harmony under a wise and beneficent ruler.

Macbeth was probably written shortly after the accession of James I and reflects the new king's interests, not only in witchcraft and Scottish history, but also in the idea of kingship itself. In his *The Trew Law of Free Monarchies* James had compared a king's duty towards his subjects with a father's love for his children, claiming that these relationships are grounded in natural law.

By the law of nature the king becomes a natural father to all his lieges at his coronation; and as the father, of his fatherly duty, is bound to care for the nourishing, education, and virtuous government of his children, even so is the king bound to care for all his subjects. As all the toil and pain that the father can take for his children will be thought light and well bestowed by him, so that the effect thereof redound to their profit and weal; so ought the prince to do towards his people. As the kindly father ought to foresee all inconvenients and dangers that may arise towards his children, and though with the hazard of his own person press to prevent the same; so ought the king towards his people. As the father's wrath and correction upon any of his children that offendeth ought to be by a fatherly chastisement seasoned with pity, as long as there is any hope of amendment in them, so ought the king towards any of his lieges that offend in that measure. And shortly, as the father's chief joy ought to be in procuring his children's welfare, rejoicing at their weal, sorrowing and pitying at their evil, to hazard for their safety, travail for their rest, wake for their sleep, and in a word, to think that his earthly felicity and life standeth and liveth more in them, nor in himself: so ought a good prince think of his people.

James VI, *The Trew Law of Free Monarchies*, pp.55-6.

The idea that love is the basis of social order goes back at least as far as Plato (c.427-348 BC) and was central to the medieval and Renaissance view of the universe. This is illustrated in the following passage from a 16th-century translation of Boethius' *The Consolation of Philosophy*, one of the most influential of all medieval philosophical works and still widely read in Elizabethan England.

The love of God that governeth both the land and the sea, and likewise commandeth the heaven, and keepeth the world in due order and good accord, that is to say, causeth the due seasons of the year to come successively according to their nature. And that the seeds, that is to say, the elements being contrary one to another do hold continual peace and unity, one with another, so that one doth not corrupt and hurt another. And that the sun in his bright golden chariot, bringeth forth the clear fresh day. And that the moon govern the night that the star Hesperus, called the evening star, hath brought in. And that the raging sea to keep in his floods, to a certain end that they extend not their uttermost course and overflow the earth. If this divine or godly love should slack the bridle, that is to say, should take no cure to govern, whatsoever thing now loveth together, and agreeth, would be at continual variance and discord, and would strive to destroy and lose the engine of the world that keepeth them in mutual amity in their goodly ordinate movings.

This love of God conserveth virtuous folk, and such as be joined together in the bond of friendship. And this love knitteth together the sacrament of wedlock, with chaste love between man and wife. This love also setteth his laws which is true friendship to faithful friends and fellows. O how happy were mankind if this love of God that ruleth heaven, might rule and govern their minds, that is to say, that they might so agree together in such perfect friendship, that one might love another, and agree as the elements do agree.

Boethius, *The Consolation of Philosophy* (AD 524, trans. 1556), p.52.

If it is the same principle which is responsible for harmony throughout the universe – among the elements, in society, between men and women – then the murder of Duncan must be seen, not simply as an act of wanton homicide, but as a violation of nature's most fundamental law. Indeed Macbeth himself knows that in betraying the king's loving trust he has made 'a breach in nature/For ruin's wasteful entrance' (II.iii.112-3).

Because the fragile bond uniting all members of society in loving trust is a mutual one it can just as easily be destroyed by a king as by his subject. Lear's rejection of Cordelia is an action which has similarly profound symbolic ramifications.

Convinced that he is 'a man/More sinn'd against than sinning' (III.ii.59-60), the aggrieved king naturally tries to minimise his faults. But although Lear is no murderer, his betrayal of his daughter's trust is shown to be just as clearly a denial of 'The offices [duties] of nature' (II.iv.177) as Macbeth's regicide. The social consequences of Lear's abrogation of his responsibility as king and father are intimated in the grotesquely barbaric images of the speech in which he rejects his daughter's love.

> *Lear.*   Now, our joy,
> Although our last and least; to whose young love
> The vines of France and milk of Burgundy
> Strive to be interess'd; what can you say to draw
> A third more opulent than your sisters? Speak.
> *Cor.* Nothing, my lord.
> *Lear.* Nothing!
> *Cor.* Nothing.
> *Lear.* Nothing will come of nothing. Speak again.
> *Cor.* Unhappy that I am, I cannot heave
> My heart unto my mouth. I love your Majesty
> According to my bond; no more nor less.
> *Lear.* How, how, Cordelia! Mend your speech a
>   little,
> Lest you may mar your fortunes.
> *Cor.*   Good, my lord,
> You have begot me, bred me, lov'd me; I
> Return those duties back as are right fit,
> Obey you, love you, and most honour you.
> Why have my sisters husbands, if they say
> They love you all? Haply, when I shall wed,
> That lord whose hand must take my plight shall carry
> Half my love with him, half my care and duty,
> Sure I shall never marry like my sisters,
> To love my father all.
> *Lear.* But goes thy heart with this?
> *Cor.*   Ay, my good lord.
> *Lear.* So young and so untender?
> *Cor.* So young, my lord, and true.
> *Lear.* Let it be so! Thy truth, then, be thy dower!
> For, by the sacred radiance of the sun,

The mysteries of Hecat and the night;
By all the operation of the orbs
From whom we do exist and cease to be;
Here I disclaim all my paternal care,
Propinquity and property of blood,
And as a stranger to my heart and me
Hold thee from this for ever. The barbarous Scythian,
Or he that makes his generation messes
To gorge his appetite, shall to my bosom
Be as well neighbour'd, pitied, and reliev'd,
As thou my sometime daughter.
Kent.   Good my liege–
Lear. Peace, Kent!
Come not between the dragon and his wrath.
I lov'd her most, and thought to set my rest
On her kind nursery. [*To Cordelia*] Hence, and avoid
    my sight!–

King Lear, I.i.81-123.

Renaissance jurists like Hooker followed the example of St Thomas Aquinas in formulating a four-fold theory of law. Their object in classifying law according to its eternal, divine, natural and human manifestations was to show that in legal, as in other matters, the human is an aspect of the divine. The clearest account in this period of the relationship between natural law and human, or positive, law is by Thomas Starkey.

Like as in many things which by experience we daily see, nature requireth the diligence of man, leaving them unperfect of themself, as the seeds and fruits of the ground, which she will never bring to perfection, if man withhold his diligence and labour; so in these virtues and law of nature, she requireth the aid and diligence of man, which else will soon be oppressed and corrupt. There be in man's life so many occasions of destroying these seeds and virtues, plants and laws, that except there be joined some good provision for their springing up and good culture, they shall never bring forth their fruit, they shall never bring man to his perfection.

Wherefore among all men and all nations, as I think, upon earth there be and ever hath been other certain customs and manners by long use and time confirmed and approved, other laws, written and devised by the politic wit of man, received and established for the maintenance and setting forward of these natural seeds and plants of virtue; which custom and law, by man so ordained and devised, is called the civil law, because they be as means to bring man to the perfection of the civil life. Without the ordinance of these laws, the other soon will be corrupt, the weeds will soon overgrow the good corn.

This law civil is far different from the other, for in every country it is diverse and variable, yea almost in every city and town. This law taketh effect of the opinion of man; it resteth wholly in his consent, and varieth according to the place and time, insomuch that in diverse time and place contrary laws are both good and both convenient to the politic life. Whereas the law of nature is ever one, in all countries, firm and stable, and never for the time varieth; it is never changeable; the consent of man doth nothing thereto; it hangeth nothing of time nor place, but according as right reason is ever one, so is this law, and never varieth after the fancy of man. This law is the ground and end of the other, to the which it must ever be referred, none otherwise than the conclusions of arts mathematical are ever referred to their principles. For civil ordinance is but as a mean to bring man to observe this law of nature, insomuch that if there be any civil law ordained which cannot be resolved thereto, it is of no value. For all good civil laws spring and issue out of the law of nature, as brooks and rivers out of fountains and wells; and to that all must be resolved and referred as to the end why they be ordained, to the observation whereof they are but as means.

Thomas Starkey, *Dialogue Between Reginald Pole and Thomas Lupset*, pp.31-2.

Starkey here makes it clear that, although customs may vary from one nation to another, nevertheless positive law is grounded on the universal rule of reason. This is the principle to which Hector appeals in the debate among the Trojan generals in the second act of *Troilus and Cressida*. The question at issue is whether or not Helen should be returned to the Greeks. Reproving Paris and Troilus for allowing themselves to be ruled by their emotions, Hector argues that the principle of reason enshrined in the law of nations demands that she be returned. But, as so often in this play, wise words are not matched by wise actions. At the end of this speech we see the defender of rationality contradicting his own principles and urging that Helen be kept in Troy on the grounds that to return her would be to compromise their 'several dignities'.

> *Hect.* Paris and Troilus, you have both said well;
> And on the cause and question now in hand
> Have gloz'd, but superficially; not much
> Unlike young men, whom Aristotle thought
> Unfit to hear moral philosophy.
> The reasons you allege do more conduce
> To the hot passion of distemp'red blood
> Than to make up a free determination
> 'Twixt right and wrong; for pleasure and revenge
> Have ears more deaf than adders to the voice
> Of any true decision. Nature craves
> All dues be rend'red to their owners. Now,
> What nearer debt in all humanity
> Than wife is to the husband? If this law
> Of nature be corrupted through affection;
> And that great minds, of partial indulgence
> To their benumbed wills, resist the same;
> There is a law in each well-order'd nation
> To curb those raging appetites that are
> Most disobedient and refractory.
> If Helen, then, be wife to Sparta's king–
> As it is known she is–these moral laws
> Of nature and of nations speak aloud
> To have her back return'd. Thus to persist
> In doing wrong extenuates not wrong,

But makes it much more heavy. Hector's opinion
Is this, in way of truth. Yet ne'er the less,
My spritely brethren, I propend to you
In resolution to keep Helen still;
For 'tis a cause that hath no mean dependence
Upon our joint and several dignities.

Troilus and Cressida, II.ii.163-93.

Legal theory played an important role in 16th-century political controversy. For example, when Robert Parsons undertakes to demolish the principle of hereditary monarchy, he bases his argument on a distinction between natural law and positive law. Although he concedes that government itself is rooted in 'an instinct of nature', Parsons claims that particular forms of government are not determined by nature, but are based on positive law and therefore open to negotiation.

These two points then are of nature, to wit, the commonwealth, and government of the same by magistrates. But what kind of government each commonwealth will have, whether *democratia,* which is popular government by the people itself, as Athens, Thebes, and many other cities of Greece had in old time, and as the Cantons of Switzers at this day have; or else *aristocratia,* which is the government of some certain chosen number of the best, as the Romans many years were governed by consuls and senators, and at this day the states of this country of Holland do imitate the same; or else *monarchia,* which is the regiment of one, and this again either of an emperor, king, duke, earl or the like: these particular forms of government, I say, are not determined by God or nature, as the other two points before, (for then they should be all one in all nations as the other are, seeing God and nature are one to all as often hath been said) but these particular forms are left unto every nation and country to choose that form of government, which they shall like best, and think most fit for the natures and conditions of their people, which Aristotle proveth throughout all the second and fourth books of his *Politics,* very largely laying down divers kinds of governments in his days, as namely in Greece that of the Milesians, Lacedemonians, Candians, and others, and showing the causes of their differences, which he attributes to the diversity of men's natures, customs, educations and other such causes that made them make choice of such or such form of government.

And this might be proved also by infinite other examples both of times past and present, and in all nations and countries both Christian and otherwise, which have not had only different fashions of governments the one from the other but even among themselves at one time, one form of government, and another at other times. For the Romans first had kings and after rejecting them for their evil government, they chose consuls, which were two governors for every year, whose authority yet they limited by a multitude of senators, which were of their counsel, and these men's power was restrained also by adding tribunes of the people, and sometimes dictators, and finally they came to be governed last of all by emperors.

> Robert Parsons, *A Conference About the Next Succession to the Crown of England* (1594), pp.9-10.

Naturally enough other writers in the period use similar legal arguments to reach different conclusions. But however much they might have disagreed in their interpretation of positive law, radicals and conservatives were, with very few exceptions, united in regarding natural law as a self-evident reality. In his *Of the Laws of Ecclesiastical Polity* Richard Hooker explains that, as something freely accessible to human reason, the law of nature is 'not agreed upon by one, or two, or few, but by all'.

> The law of reason or human nature is that which men by discourse of natural reason have rightly found out themselves to be all for ever bound unto in their actions.

Laws of reason have these marks to be known by. Such as keep them resemble most lively in their voluntary actions that very manner of working which nature herself doth necessarily observe in the course of the whole world. The works of nature are all behoveful, beautiful, without superfluity or defect; even so theirs, if they be framed according to that which the law of reason teacheth. Secondly, those laws are investigable by reason, without the help of revelation supernatural and divine. Finally, in such sort they are investigable, that the knowledge of them is general, the world hath always been acquainted with them; according to that which one in Sophocles observeth concerning a branch of this law, 'It is no child of to-day's or yesterday's birth, but hath been no man knoweth how long sithence [ago]'. It is not agreed upon by one, or two, or few, but by all. Which we may not so understand, as if every particular man in the whole world did know and confess whatsoever the law of reason doth contain; but this law is such that being proposed no man can reject it as unreasonable and unjust. Again, there is nothing in it but any man (having natural perfection of wit and ripeness of judgement) may by labour and travail find out. And to conclude, the general principles thereof are such, as it is not easy to find men ignorant of them. Law rational therefore, which men commonly use to call the law of nature, meaning thereby the law which human nature knoweth itself in reason universally bound unto, which also for that cause may be termed most fitly the law of reason; this law, I say, comprehendeth all those things which men by the light of their natural understanding evidently know, or at leastwise may know, to be beseeming or unbeseeming, virtuous or vicious, good or evil for them to do.

Richard Hooker, *Of the Laws of Ecclesiastical Polity* (1594-7), Vol. I,p.182.

In asserting the power of human reason to participate in divine law Hooker, like Starkey before him, is making an emphatic claim for man's dignity and rationality. However, from the early years of the 16th century this rationalistic view of human nature had been challenged from two different quarters. Approaching the question of man's essential nature from diametrically opposed points of view, Calvin and Machiavelli offered equally devastating threats to the commonplaces of Renaissance thought. Where Machiavelli simply ignores the whole edifice of natural law, setting out with uncompromising frankness the unsavoury realities of human nature, Calvin openly confronts the theory of human dignity. In his view natural law is inscrutable, confirming man not in the excellency of his reason, but in his imbecility (*The Institution of Christian Religion*, II.viii.1).

Of these two it is Machiavelli's coolly pragmatic view of human nature which left its mark more clearly in Shakespeare's plays. In his *Discourses on Livy's History of Rome* Machiavelli gives an account of the origin of human society which is in sharp contrast to Starkey's Christian humanism. For him it is not a naturally implanted desire for 'civil order and loving company' which impels man to form civil communities, but fear and self-interest.

> Intending then to treat what were the ordinances of the city of Rome, and the accidents that brought it to perfection, I say, that some, who have writ of commonwealths, will have it, that then was one of these three kinds of state termed by them a principality, another an aristocracy, and a third a popular government, and that they who lay the first grounds of rule and order in a city ought most to have regard to some one of these, as it seems fittest to their purpose. Some others (and that following the opinion of many more wise) think that there be six sorts of governments, of which three are bad in extremity, and three good in themselves but so easy to be corrupted, that even they become pernicious. Those which are good, are the three aforesaid; the bad are the other three which depend on these, and every one of them in such sort resembles that which it approaches, that they change suddenly from one into the other: for the principality easily becomes tyranny, that of the

nobility falls into the hands of some few, and the popular will as easily become tumultuous: so that if he that lays the foundation of a commonwealth ordains in a city one of the three sorts, it is but for a small continuance. For it is beyond the power of any remedy to hinder that it slip not into its contrary, for the resemblance which in this case there is between the virtue and the vice. These differences of governments grew by chance among men. For in the beginning of the world, when the inhabitants were lone, they were scattered abroad for a time like wild beasts. Afterwards mankind increasing, they gathered together, and that they might be able better to defend themselves, they began to cast their eyes upon him who had the most strength and courage among them, and made him their head and obeyed him. Hereupon began the discerning of things good and honest, from bad and hurtful: for seeing that anyone hurt his benefactor, it caused hatred and pity among men, blaming the ungrateful and honouring the thankful, and thinking withal that the same injuries might as well be done to themselves, to avoid the like evil, they betook them to make laws and to make punishments against the offenders. Hence came the knowledge of justice, which was the occasion that when they were to choose a prince they sought not after him that was the lustiest but the wisest and justest.

Niccolo Machiavelli, *Machiavels Discourses upon the first Decade of T. Livius*, (c.1520, trans. 1636), pp.10-11.

With complete indifference to the theological premises on which most medieval and Renaissance political theory rested, Machiavelli portrays a harshly competitive world in which man's aggressive and acquisitive instincts have no natural bounds. It is a view of human nature not far removed from that of Shakespeare's Edmund.

Edm. Thou, Nature, art my goddess; to thy law
My services are bound. Wherefore should I
Stand in the plague of custom, and permit

> The curiosity of nations to deprive me,
> For that I am some twelve or fourteen moonshines
> Lag of a brother? Why bastard? Wherefore base?
> When my dimensions are as well compact,
> My mind as generous, and my shape as true,
> As honest madam's issue? Why brand they us
> With base? with baseness? bastardy? base, base?
> Who, in the lusty stealth of nature, take
> More composition and fierce quality
> Than doth, within a dull, stale, tired bed,
> Go to th' creating a whole tribe of fops
> Got 'tween asleep and wake? Well then,
> Legitimate Edgar, I must have your land.
> Our father's love is to the bastard Edmund
> As to th' legitimate. Fine word 'legitimate'!
> Well, my legitimate, if this letter speed,
> And my invention thrive, Edmund the base
> Shall top th' legitimate. I grow; I prosper.
> Now, gods, stand up for bastards.

King Lear, I.ii.1-22.

By demythologising nature Machiavelli had implied that our ideas of social justice, far from being immutable and incontestable, are in fact arbitrary. The implications of such subjectivist arguments were deeply disturbing. Already by the 1530s we find Thomas Starkey warning of the 'pestilent persuasion of them which say and affirm betwixt vice and virtue no difference to be but only strong opinion and fancy' (p.33). By the middle of the 17th century natural law had begun to lose its old meaning of certain God-given duties and obligations and for some thinkers now meant 'the liberty of each man hath, to use his own power, as he will himself, for the preservation of his own nature' (Hobbes, *Leviathan*, Chapter XIV). John Donne's complaint in a famous passage from *An Anatomy of the World* that the 'new Philosophy calls all in doubt' may be taken as a measure of the intellectual uncertainty of the age.

> As mankind, so is the world's whole frame
> Quite out of joint, almost created lame:
> For, before God had made up all the rest,

Corruption entered, and depraved the best:
It seized the angels, and then first of all
The world did in her cradle take a fall,
And turned her brains, and took a general maim
Wronging each joint of th' universal frame.
The noblest part, man, felt it first; and then
Both beasts and plants, cursed in the curse of man.
So did the world from the first hour decay,
That evening was beginning of the day,
And now the springs and summers which we see,
Like sons of women after fifty be.
And new philosophy calls in all doubt,
The element of fire is quite put out;
The sun is lost, and th' earth, and no man's wit
Can well direct him where to look for it.
And freely men confess that this world's spent,
When in the planets, and the firmament
They seek so many new; they see that this
Is crumbled out again to his atomies.
'Tis all in pieces, all coherence gone;
All just supply, and all relation:
Prince, subject, father, son, are things forgot,
For every man alone thinks he hath got
To be a phoenix, and that then can be
None of that kind, of which he is, but he.
This is the world's condition now.

> John Donne, *An Anatomy of the World* (1611),
> ll.191-219.

The sense of the confusion of values which led Donne to admit that 'this term the "law of nature" is so variously and inconstantly delivered, as I confess I read it a hundred times before I understood it once' (*Biathanatos*, p.52) is mirrored in the intellectual dilemmas of Shakespeare's tragic heroes and heroines. In Hamlet's case the ostensible problem is one which had been exhaustively debated throughout the 16th century – how to deal with a tyrant. However, such is the turmoil which reigns in the 'distracted globe' (I.v.97) of Hamlet's mind that he is quickly diverted from the problem of whether or not to resist tyranny to the question of suicide.

Ham. To be, or not to be–that is the question;
Whether 'tis nobler in the mind to suffer
The slings and arrows of outrageous fortune,
Or to take arms against a sea of troubles,
And by opposing end them? To die, to sleep–
No more; and by a sleep to say we end
The heart-ache and the thousand natural shocks
That flesh is heir to. 'Tis a consummation
Devoutly to be wish'd. To die, to sleep;
To sleep, perchance to dream. Ay, there's the rub;
For in that sleep of death what dreams may come,
When we have shuffled off this mortal coil,
Must give us pause. There's the respect
That makes calamity of so long life;
For who would bear the whips and scorns of time,
Th' oppressor's wrong, the proud man's contumely,
The pangs of despis'd love, the law's delay,
The insolence of office, and the spurns
That patient merit of th' unworthy takes,
When he himself might his quietus make
With a bare bodkin? Who would these fardels bear,
To grunt and sweat under a weary life,
But that the dread of something after death–
The undiscover'd country, from whose bourn
No traveller returns–puzzles the will,
And makes us rather bear those ills we have
Than fly to others that we know not of?
Thus conscience does make cowards of us all;
And thus the native hue of resolution
Is sicklied o'er with the pale cast of thought,
And enterprises of great pitch and moment,
With this regard, their currents turn awry
And lose the name of action.

Hamlet, III.i.56-88.

The problem of reconciling the demands of natural law
with those of a personal code of honour when the two are
apparently in conflict is a classic formula for tragedy. But it
would be too easy simply to say that Hamlet errs in allowing
his emotions to become 'Lord of his reason' (*Antony and
Cleopatra*, III.xiii.4). The cause of his paralysis of will is not

simply a question of competing demands on his conscience: it is also a sense that the rational stoicism he professes to admire is helpless in the Machiavellian world of the Danish court. In *Hamlet* we have the paradox of a philosopher who not only suspects that 'there is nothing either good or bad but thinking makes it so' (II.ii.249-50), but who confesses that he 'cannot reason' (II.ii.264).

King Lear offers a similarly sceptical view of human rationality. Dividing his cast with almost diagrammatic symmetry into groups of good and evil, Shakespeare appears to endorse the values of the virtuous characters only to expose the illusoriness of their intellectual convictions. In the last and most painful scene of the play we see the mild and gentle Albany respond first with pious outrage as the bodies of Goneril and Regan are brought on stage, then with anxious prayer as he discovers that Cordelia's life is also in danger and finally with despair as he discovers that she too is already dead. But Albany's repeated appeals to a providence who punishes the wicked and protects the innocent are shown to be as naive as Gloucester's belief in the influence of the stars.

> *Enter a* Gentleman *with a bloody knife.*
> *Gent.* Help, help, O, help!
> *Edg.*   What kind of help?
> *Alb.* Speak, man.
> *Edg.* What means this bloody knife?
> *Gent.*   'Tis hot, it smokes;
> It came even from the heart of–O, she's dead!
> *Alb.* Who dead? Speak, man.
> *Gent.* Your lady, sir, your lady! and her sister
> By her is poison'd; she confesses it.
> *Edm.* I was contracted to them both. All three
> Now marry in an instant.
> *Edg.*   Here comes Kent.
>
>   *Enter* Kent.
>
> *Alb.* Produce the bodies, be they alive or dead. [*Exit Gentleman.*]
> This judgement of the heavens, that makes us tremble,
> Touches us not with pity. O, is this he?
> The time will not allow the compliment

Which very manners urges.

Kent.   I am come
To bid my king and master aye good night.
Is he not here?

Alb.   Great thing of us forgot!
Speak, Edmund, where's the King? and where's
    Cordelia? [*The bodies of Goneril and Regan are
    brought in.*]
See'st thou this object, Kent?

Kent. Alack, why thus?

Edm.   Yet Edmund was belov'd.
The one the other poison'd for my sake,
And after slew herself.

Alb. Even so. Cover their faces.

Edm. I pant for life. Some good I mean to do,
Despite of mine own nature. Quickly send—
Be brief in it—to th' castle; for my writ
Is on the life of Lear and on Cordelia.
Nay, send in time.

Alb.   Run, run, O, run!

Edg. To who, my lord? Who has the office? Send
Thy token of reprieve.

Edm. Well thought on. Take my sword;
Give it to the Captain.

Alb.   Haste thee, for thy life.
[*Exit Edgar.*]

Edm. He hath commission from thy wife and me
To hang Cordelia in the prison, and
To lay the blame upon her own despair,
That she fordid herself.

Alb. The gods defend her! Bear him hence awhile.
[*Edmund is borne off.*]

Enter Lear, *with* Cordelia *dead in his arms;* Edgar,
    Captain *and* Others *following.*

Lear. Howl, howl, howl, howl! O, you are men of
    stones!
Had I your tongues and eyes, I'd use them so
That heaven's vault should crack. She's gone for ever.
I know when one is dead and when one lives;
She's dead as earth. Lend me a looking-glass;
If that her breath will mist or stain the stone,

Why, then she lives.
Kent.   Is this the promis'd end?
Edg. Or image of that horror?
Alb.   Fall and cease!

King Lear, V.iii.222-64.

In portraying a world in which only fools and innocents are truly wise Shakespeare seems to share the views of the sceptical Montaigne, whose *Essays* were first translated into English in 1603 shortly before Shakespeare wrote *King Lear*. In the celebrated essay entitled 'Apology for Raimond Sebond' Montaigne argues that all metaphysical speculation is simply self-indulgent fantasy, and that natural law, far from being freely accessible to reason, is essentially unknowable.

> Presumption is our natural and original infirmity. Of all creatures, man is the most miserable and frail, and therewithal the proudest and disdainfullest. Who perceiveth and seeth himself placed here, amidst the filth and mire of the world, fast tied and nailed to the worst, most senseless, and drooping part of the world, in the vilest corner of the house, and farthest from heaven's cope, with those creatures that are the worst of the three conditions; and yet dareth imaginarily place himself above the circle of the moon, and reduce heaven under his feet. It is through the vanity of the same imagination, that he dare equal himself to God, that he ascribeth divine conditions unto himself, that he selecteth and separateth himself from out the rank of other creatures to which his fellow-brethren and compeers, he cuts out and shareth their parts, and allotteth them what portion of means or forces he thinks good. How knoweth he by the virtue of his understanding the inward and secret motions of beasts? By what comparison from them to us doth he conclude the brutishness he ascribeth unto them? . . . It is not long of a true discourse, but of a foolish-hardiness, and self-presuming obstinacy, we prefer ourselves before other creatures, and sequester ourselves from their condition and society. But to return to our purpose, we have for our part in

constancy, irresolution, uncertainty, sorrow, superstition, carefulness, for future things (yea after our
life) ambition, covetousness, jealousy, envy, inordin-
ate, mad and untamed appetites, war, falsehood,
disloyalty, detraction, and curiosity. Surely we have
strangely overpaid this worthy discourse, whereof we
so much glory, and this readiness to judge, or capacity
to know, if we have purchased the same with the price
of so infinite passions, to which we are incessantly
enthralled. . . . Hath God delivered into our hands the
keys, and the strongest wards of His infinite
puissance? Hath He obliged Himself not to exceed
the bounds of our knowledge? Suppose, oh man, that
herein thou hast been able to mark some signs of His
effects. Thinkest thou He hath therein employed all
He was able to do, and that He hath placed all His
forms and ideas, in this piece of work? Thou seest but
the order and policy of this little, little cell wherein
thou art placed. The question is, whither thou seest it.
His divinity hath an infinite jurisdiction far beyond
that. This piece is nothing in respect of the whole.
This law [natural law] thou allegest is but a municipal
law, and thou knowest not what the universal is.

> Michel de Montaigne, 'Apology for Raimond
> Sebond', *The Essays*, pp.260-303 (abridged).

At a time of violent collision between traditional and
radical ideas Shakespeare's plays reflect through their
dialectical structures of opposing beliefs and attitudes 'the
very age and body of the time his form and pressure'
(*Hamlet*, III.ii.24-5). Declaring by means of images of
barbarism and insanity the terrible consequences which must
inevitably follow the violation of natural law, plays like
Hamlet and *King Lear* reveal, at the same time, a world in
which providence, if it exists, is inscrutable and human reason
pitifully ineffectual. The closest that Shakespeare comes to
what might be called a personal testament is in his last play,
The Tempest; though even here political questions are dealt
with in a typically oblique and elusive manner.

The Tempest recapitulates in microcosm most of the major

political themes of the histories and tragedies: the limitations of man's fallen nature; alternative forms of government; the remiss ruler; the just monarch; the problem of rebellion; the nature of providence. It offers a vision of order and harmony in which the disparate elements of society are united, or at least controlled by the rule of a beneficent autocrat whose apparent harshness belies a true compassion. With its romantic plot and fairy-tale ending this play may seem close to sentimental escapism. But Shakespeare is careful, by means of various self-reflexive dramatic devices, to make it clear that this vision is to be seen, not as a mirror image of reality, but as a hypothesis. One such device is Prospero's masque in Act IV. Before Prospero will allow his daughter and her lover to consummate their union he arranges a spectacle in which nymphs and goddesses join in conferring their blessings on the young couple.

Cer.   Highest Queen of state,
Great Juno, comes; I know her by her gait.
Juno. How does my bounteous sister? Go with me
To bless this twain, that they may prosperous be,
And honour'd in their issue.

They sing.

Juno. Honour, riches, marriage-blessing,
    Long continuance, and increasing,
    Hourly joys be still upon you!
    Juno sings her blessing on you.

Cer. Earth's increase, foison plenty,
    Barns and garners never empty;
    Vines with clust'ring bunches growing,
    Plants with goodly burden bowing;
    Spring come to you at the farthest,
    In the very end of harvest!
    Scarcity and want shall shun you,
    Ceres' blessing so is on you.

Fer. This is a most majestic vision, and
Harmonious charmingly. May I be bold

To think these spirits?
Pro.   Spirits, which by mine art
I have from their confines call'd to enact
My present fancies.
Fer.   Let me live here ever;
So rare a wond'red father and a wise
Makes this place Paradise.
[*Juno and Ceres whisper, and send Iris on
employment.*]
Pro.   Sweet now, silence;
Juno and Ceres whisper seriously.
There's something else to do; hush, and be mute,
Or else our spell is marr'd.
Iris. You nymphs, call'd Naiads, of the wind'ring
brooks,
With your sedg'd crowns and ever harmless looks,
Leave your crisp channels, and on this green land
Answer your summons; Juno does command.
Come, temperate nymphs, and help to celebrate
A contract of true love; be not too late.

Enter certain Nymphs.

You sun-burnt sicklemen, of August weary,
Come hither from the furrow, and be merry;
Make holiday; your rye-straw hats put on,
And these fresh nymphs encounter every one
In country footing.

Enter certain Reapers, *properly habited; they join
with the Nymphs in a graceful dance; towards the end
whereof Prospero starts suddenly, and speaks; after
which, to a strange, hollow, and confused noise, they
heavily vanish.*

Pro. [*Aside*] I had forgot that foul conspiracy
Of the beast Caliban and his confederates
Against my life; the minute of their plot
Is almost come. [*To the Spirits*] Well done; avoid; no
more!
Fer. This is strange; your father's in some passion

That works him strongly.
Mira.   Never till this day
Saw I him touch'd with anger so distemper'd.
Pro. You do look, my son, in a mov'd sort,
As if you were dismay'd; be cheerful, sir.
Our revels now are ended. These our actors,
As I foretold you, were all spirits, and
Are melted into air, into thin air;
And, like the baseless fabric of this vision,
The cloud-capp'd towers, the gorgeous palaces,
The solemn temples, the great globe itself,
Yea, all which it inherit, shall dissolve,
And, like this insubstantial pageant faded,
Leave not a rack behind. We are such stuff
As dreams are made on; and our little life
Is rounded with a sleep. Sir, I am vex'd;
Bear with my weakness; my old brain is troubled;
Be not disturb'd with my infirmity.
If you be pleas'd, retire into my cell
And there repose;

The Tempest, IV.i.101-162.

Spellbound by this vision of Golden-Age harmony where spring and summer, generation and harvest occur simultaneously, Ferdinand imagines he has found a paradise on earth. But the substance of Juno's song is no more an attainable reality than that of Shakespeare's play: both are 'insubstantial pageants'.

The Tempest is neither a utopia nor a dystopia, but something less sensational than either of these. By calling attention to its own dramatic nature the play serves both as a warning that utopian dreams are idle and ultimately destructive, and also as an expression of a belief that a limited degree of harmony may be achieved in an ineluctably imperfect world. Whether or not that vision of social harmony can ever be achieved depends finally on us, the audience. That is why Prospero, in the play's epilogue, must supplicate for applause. If we approve his vision, it will have done its work and the author will be free to resign his awesome responsibility; if we do not, the 'project fails'.

Chronological Table

Date	Contemporary events	Shakespeare's plays (approximate dates of first performances)	Other notable literary and publishing events
1558	Accession of Elizabeth I		
1559			William Baldwin (ed.), *The Mirror for Magistrates*
1560			Geneva Bible; Thirty-nine Articles
1561			English trans. of Calvin's *Institutes*
1563			John Foxe, *Book of Martyrs*
1564	Birth of Shakespeare		
1567	Revolt of the Netherlands		
1569	Northern Rebellion		
1570	Elizabeth I excommunicated by the Pope; Ridolfi plot exposed		*An Homilie Agaynst Disobedience and Wylful Rebellion*
1571	Defeat of the Turks at Battle of Lepanto		
1572	Massacre of St Bartholomew's Day		
1576		'The Theatre', Shoreditch opened	

Date	Contemporary events	Shakespeare's plays (approximate dates of first performances)	Other notable literary and publishing events
1579			English trans. of *Plutarch's Lives* (Sir Thomas North)
1582	Plague in London		
1583			Sir Thomas Smith, *De Republica Anglorum* (written 1562-5) published
1584			Machiavelli's *The Prince* pub. in London in Italian
1587	Execution of Mary Queen of Scots		Holinshed's *Chronicles* (revised edn)
1588	Spanish Armada defeated		'Martin Marprelate' controversy (1588-90)
1590			Sir Philip Sidney, *Arcadia;* Edmund Spenser, *The Faerie Queene*, Bks I-III
1591		*Henry VI*, Pts 2 & 3	
1592	Plague in London; playhouses closed	*Henry VI*, Pt 1	
1593		*Richard III*	
1594			Hooker's *Laws of Ecclesiastical Polity*, vols 1-4 (vol. 5 pub. 1597); English trans. of Lipsius' *Six Bookes of Politickes*
1595	Rebellion in Ireland	*Richard II; Romeo and Juliet*	

Date	Contemporary events	Shakespeare's plays (approximate dates of first performances)	Other notable literary and publishing events
1596	Swan Theatre, Bankside opened	*King John*	Edmund Spenser, *The Faerie Queene*, Bks IV-VI
1597	Second Armada dispersed	*Henry IV*, Pts 1 & 2	
1598			James VI, *The Trew Law of Free Monarchies*
1599	Globe Theatre, Bankside opened	*Henry V; Julius Caesar*	English trans. of Contarini's *Commonwealth and Government of Venice*
1600	Second Blackfriars Theatre opened		
1601	Essex rebellion; Irish rebellion suppressed	*Hamlet*	
1602		*Troilus and Cressida*	
1603	Death of Elizabeth I; accession of James I (1603-25); plague in London		English trans. of Montaigne's *Essays* (John Florio); Richard Knolles, *The Generall Historie of the Turkes*
1604	Hampton Court Conference; peace with Spain	*Othello; Measure for Measure*	
1605	Gunpowder Plot discovered	*King Lear*	
1606		*Macbeth*	English trans. of Bodin's *The Six Bookes of a Commonweale*
1607	Revolt in the Midlands over corn shortages	*Antony and Cleopatra*	

Date	Contemporary events	Shakespeare's plays (approximate date of first performances)	Other notable literary and publishing events
1608	'The King's Men' take over second Blackfriars Theatre	*Coriolanus*	
1609	Virginia Company expedition wrecked off Bermuda		
1610		*The Winter's Tale*	
1611		*The Tempest*	King James Bible; John Donne, *The First Anniversary*
1613		*Henry VIII* (probably in collaboration with John Fletcher)	
1616	Death of Shakespeare		

Bibliography

PRIMARY SOURCES

Amyot, Jaques, Preface to Plutarch's *Lives of the Noble Grecians and Romans* (1559), trans. Sir Thomas North (1579), ed. George Wyndham, 6 vols (London, 1895-6)

Aylmer, John, *An Harborowe for Faithfull and Trewe Subjectes* (London, 1559)

Baldwin, William (ed), *The Mirror for Magistrates* (1563), ed. Lily B. Campbell (Cambridge, 1938; rpt New York, 1960)

Bodin, Jean, *The Six Bookes of a Commonweale* (1576), trans. Richard Knolles (1606), facsimile edn, Kenneth Douglas McRae (Cambridge, Mass., 1962)

Boethius, *The Consolation of Philosophy* (AD 524), trans. George Colville (1556), ed. Ernest Belfort Bax (London, 1897)

Calendar of State Papers (Venice 1592-1603)

Calvin, Jean, *The Institution of Christian Religion* (1535), trans. Thomas Norton (1561; rpt London, 1599)

Charron, Pierre, *Of Wisdome* (1601), trans. Samson Lennard (London, 1606)

Contarini, Gaspar, *The Commonwealth and Government of Venice* (1543), trans. Lewes Lewkenor (London, 1599)

Cooper, Thomas, *An Admonition to the People of England* (1589), ed. Edward Arber (London, 1895)

Donne, John, *Biathanatos,* Modern Spelling edn, ed. Michael Rudick and M. Pabst Battin (New York and London, 1982)

— *The Complete English Poems,* ed. A.J. Smith (Harmondsworth, 1971)

Elton, G.R., ed., *The Tudor Constitution: Documents and Commentary* (Cambridge, 1960)

Elyot, Sir Thomas, *The Boke Named The Governour* (1531), Everyman Library (London, 1907)

Erasmus, Desiderius, *The Education of a Christian Prince* (1516), trans. Lester K. Born (New York, 1936)

Fulbecke, William, *The Pandectes of the Law of Nations* (London, 1602)

Gentillet, Innocent, *A Discourse upon the Meanes of Wel Governing . . . Against Nicholas Machiavell* (1576), trans. Simon Patericke (London, 1602)

Hall, Edward, *The Union of the Two Noble and Illustre Families of Lancaster and York (Hall's Chronicle)* (London 1548; rpt London 1809)

Hayward, Sir John, *An Answer to the First Part of a Certaine Conference Concerning Succession* (London, 1603)

Holinshed, Raphael, *Chronicles of England, Scotland, and Ireland* (1577) revised edn (1587) by John Hooker, 6 vols (1587; rpt London, 1807)

An Homilie Agaynst Disobedience and Wylful Rebellion (London, 1570)

Hooker, Richard, *Of the Laws of Ecclesiastical Polity* (1594-7) Everyman Library, 2 vols (London, 1907)

James VI, (James I of England), *The Trew Law of Free Monarchies: Or the Reciprock and Mutuall Duetie Betwixt a Free King, and his Natural Subjects* (1598), *The Political Works of James I*, ed. Charles Howard McIlwain (New York, 1965)

Knolles, Richard, *The Generall Historie of the Turkes* (1603), 2nd edn (London, 1610)

Lipsius, Justus, *Six Bookes of Politickes or Civil Doctrine* (1589), trans. William Jones (London, 1594)

Lyly, John, *Euphues and His England* (1580), *The Complete Works of John Lyly*, ed. R. Warwick Bond, 3 vols (Oxford, 1902), vol. II, pp.1-228

Machiavelli, Niccolo, *Machiavels Discourses upon the first Decade of T. Livius* (c.1520), trans. Edward Dacres (London, 1636)

— *The Prince* (1514), trans. Edward Dacres (1640), Tudor Translations (London, 1905)

Merbury, Charles, *A Brief Discourse of Royal Monarchy, as of the Best Commonweal* (London, 1581)

Montaigne, Michel de, *The Essays* (1588), trans. John Florio (London, 1603)

Ovid, *Shakespeare's Ovid: Being Arthur Golding's Translation of the 'Metamorphoses'*, ed. W.H.D. Rouse (London, 1961)

Parsons, Robert, *A Conference About the Next Succession to the Crown of England* (London, 1594)

Pico della Mirandola, Giovanni, 'Oration on The Dignity of Man' (1486), trans. Elizabeth Livermore Forbes, in *The Renaissance Philosophy of Man*, eds. Ernst Cassirer, Paul Oskar Kristeller and John Herman Randall, Jr (Chicago, 1948), pp.223-54

Plowden, Edmund, *The Commentaries or Reports of Edmund Plowden* (1578), 2 vols (London, 1916)

Ponet, John, *A Short Treatise of Politic Power*, (1556) facsimile edn (Menston, 1970)

Puttenham, George, *The Arte of English Poesie* (1589), facsimile edn (Menston, 1968)

Shakespeare, William, *The Complete Works*, ed. Peter Alexander
    (London, 1951)
Smith, Sir Thomas, *De Republica Anglorum* (1583), ed. Mary
    Dewar (Cambridge, 1982)
Spenser, Edmund, *The Poetical Works of Edmund Spenser*, ed. J.C.
    Smith and E. de Selincourt (London, 1912)
Starkey, Thomas, *Dialogue Between Reginald Pole and Thomas
    Lupset* (c.1534) ed. K.M. Burton (London, 1948)
Thomas Aquinas, Saint, *On Kingship: To the King of Cyprus* (1266),
    trans. Gerald B. Phelan, revised edn I.Th. Eschmann, O.P.
    (Toronto, 1949)

SECONDARY SOURCES

In addition to the critical and scholarly works cited in the text, the following list includes a selection of books on Elizabethan and Jacobean history, Renaissance political theory and Shakespeare. For a survey of modern criticism of Shakespeare's historical and political plays see Robin Headlam Wells, 'The Fortunes of Tillyard: Twentieth-Century Critical Debate on Shakespeare's History Plays', *English Studies*, 66 (1985), pp.391-403.

Allen, J.W., *A History of Political Thought in the Sixteenth Century*
    (London, 1928)
Baumer, Franklin le van, *The Early Tudor Theory of Kingship*
    (1940; rpt New York, 1966)
Bevington, David, *Tudor Drama and Politics: A Critical Approach
    to Topical Meaning* (Cambridge, Mass., 1968)
Birch, Thomas, *The Court and Times of James the First*, 2 vols
    (London, 1848)
Dollimore, Jonathan, *Radical Tragedy: Religion, Ideology and
    Power in the Drama of Shakespeare and his Contemporaries*
    (Brighton, 1984)
Dollimore, Jonathan and Sinfield, Alan, (eds.), *Political
    Shakespeare: New Essays in Cultural Materialism* (Manchester,
    1985)
Drakakis, John, (ed.), *Alternative Shakespeares* (London, 1985)
Elton, G.R., *England Under the Tudors*, 2nd edn, (London, 1974)
Fink, Z.S., *The Classical Republicans: An Essay in the Recovery of a
    Pattern of Thought in Seventeenth-Century England*, 2nd edn
    (Evanston, Ill., 1962)
Gurr, Andrew, '*Henry V* and the Bees' Commonwealth',
    Shakespeare Survey, 30 (1977), pp.61-72

Haydn, Hiram, *The Counter-Renaissance* (New York, 1950)
Heilman, Robert B., 'Shakespearean Comedy and Tragedy: Implicit
    Political Analogies' in *Shakespeare as Political Thinker*, eds.
    John Alvis and Thomas G. West (Durham, N.C., 1981),
    pp.27-37
Hirst, Derek, *The Representatives of the People? Voters and Voting
    in England under the Early Stuarts* (Cambridge, 1975)
Johnson, Samuel, *Preface to Shakespeare, The Works of Samuel
    Johnson*, vol. VII of Yale edn, ed. Arthur Sherbo (New Haven
    and London, 1968), pp.59-113
Judson, Margaret Atwood, *The Crisis of the Constitution: An Essay
    in Constitutional and Political Thought in England 1603-1645*
    (New York, 1949)
Kantorowicz, Ernst H., *The King's Two Bodies: A Study in
    Medieval Political Theology* (Princeton, 1957)
Kelly, Henry Ansgar, *Divine Providence in the England of
    Shakespeare's Histories* (Cambridge, Mass., 1970)
Kenyon, J.P., ed., *The Stuart Constitution 1603-1688: Documents
    and Commentary* (Cambridge, 1966)
Kott, Jan, *Shakespeare Our Contemporary*, trans. Boleslaw
    Taborski (London, 1964)
Levy, F.J., *Tudor Historical Thought* (San Marino, 1967)
Morris, Christopher, *Political Thought in England: Tyndale to
    Hooker* (London, 1953)
Neale, J.E., *Elizabeth I and her Parliaments 1559-1581*, 2 vols
    (London, 1953-7)
— *Queen Elizabeth* (London, 1934)
Ornstein, Robert, *A Kingdom For a Stage: The Achievement of
    Shakespeare's History Plays* (Cambridge, Mass., 1972)
Palmer, John, *Political Characters of Shakespeare* (1945), rpt in
    Political and Comic Characters in Shakespeare (London, 1962)
Patrides, C.A., '"The Beast with Many Heads": Renaissance Views
    on the Multitude', *Shakespeare Quarterly*, 16 (1965), pp.241-46
Pettet, E.C., '*Coriolanus* and the Midlands Insurrection of 1607',
    Shakespeare Survey, 3 (1950), pp.34-42
Phillips, James Emerson, Jr, *The State in Shakespeare's Greek and
    Roman Plays* (1940, rpt New York, 1972)
Prior, Moody E., *The Drama of Power: Studies in Shakespeare's
    History Plays* (Evanston, Ill., 1973)
Raab, Felix, *The English Face of Machiavelli: A Changing
    Interpretation 1500-1700* (London, 1964)
Reed, Robert Rentoul, Jr, *Crime and God's Punishment in
    Shakespeare* (Lexington, 1984)
Ribner, Irving, *The English History Play in the Age of Shakespeare*
    (1957), revised edn (London, 1965)

Rossiter, A.P., 'Ambivalence: The Dialectic of the Histories' in *Angel with Horns: Fifteen Lectures on Shakespeare*, ed. Graham Storey (London, 1971), pp.40-64

Rowse, A.L., *William Shakespeare: A Biography* (London, 1963)

Russell, Conrad, *The Crisis of Parliaments: English History 1509-1660* (London, 1971)

Sabine, George H., *A History of Political Theory* (1937) (3rd edn London, 1963)

Sanders, Wilbur, *The Dramatist and the Received Idea: Studies in the Plays of Marlowe and Shakespeare* (Cambridge, 1968)

Stone, Lawrence, *The Causes of the English Revolution 1529-1642* (London, 1972)

Talbert, Ernest William, *The Problem of Order: Elizabethan Political Commonplaces and an Example of Shakespeare's Art* (Chapel Hill, 1962)

Tillyard, E.M.W., *Shakespeare's History Plays* (1944; rpt Harmondsworth, 1962)

Wilders, John, *The Lost Garden: A View of Shakespeare's English and Roman History Plays* (London, 1978)

Zeeveld, W. Gordon, '*Coriolanus* and Jacobean Politics', *Modern Language Review*, 57 (1962), pp.321-34

— *The Foundations of Tudor Policy* (Cambridge, Mass., 1948)

Index